A FAMILY ALBUM

A Family Album

BY REBEKAH BAINES JOHNSON

INTRODUCTION BY
PRESIDENT LYNDON BAINES JOHNSON

EDITED BY JOHN S. MOURSUND

McGraw-Hill Book Company / New York / Toronto / London

Library of Congress Catalog Card Number: 65–25547

FIRST EDITION   32661

ACKNOWLEDGMENTS

Excerpts from the following publications are reprinted by permission:
Handbook of Texas, reprinted with permission of the State Historical Association,
Austin, Texas. *Heroines of the Hills of Southwest Texas* by Dean T. U. Taylor,
reprinted with permission of the *Frontier Times*, Bandera, Texas. *Trail Drivers of
Texas*, compiled by J. Marvin Hunter, reprinted with permission of
Mrs. John V. Saul.

To Lyndon,
my beloved son, in whom I find the best
of all who have gone before.

With dearest love and fondest hopes,

Mother.

May this ancestral history be of interest
as a record of the lives that have gone
into the making of your life, afford you
fuller understanding of the traits of mind
and heart which are your inheritance, and
inspire you to greater heights.

Christmas 1954

Contents

April 7, 1965

Dear Sirs,

As you may know, my mother before her death wrote, and gave to me for Christmas in 1954, a book containing facts concerning my forebears, photographs and other items relating to the family. Those who have seen the book are impressed with its historical interest. Accordingly, it seemed to me that in view of the Foundation's interest in the history of the area in which it operates, the book should be owned by The Johnson City Foundation.

I, therefore, donate to you herewith all my right, title and interest in this manuscript, which is sometimes referred to as "Mother's Album," for such uses as the Trustees of the Foundation shall deem appropriate. This gift is to be effective at once.

As we grow older, our eyes turn with more respectful attention and warm interest to our beginnings and I see once more my mother's life as she wrote of those pioneers and travelers westward who formed the lives of today's generation.

You who knew my mother well can share the pride with me that her beautiful prose may be enjoyed by many others. She loved her family, and loved writing and in this album she brings together the things she held most dear.

I remember so well her writing the copy and selling the ads, and setting up the print for the Johnson City Record-Courier.

For love of words -- and to help the family income -- she took on other modest writing assignments -- "stringer" for several newspapers.

Board of Trustees   April 7, 1965

    Every day of my life she helped me. I am grateful that
with this gift I am able to provide her work a wider circulation.

    I am grateful for the opportunity to share this family
album with other families. I hope they will be strengthened
by it as my family has been.

                    Sincerely,

                    Lyndon B. Johnson

Board of Trustees
The Johnson City Foundation
Johnson City, Texas

It is obvious that in the field of local history and in many family histories one will find a certain number of historical inaccuracies. The basic reasons for this are that hearsay, recollections and reminiscences of happenings have been passed on from one generation to another, and that when newspapers report these happenings of a bygone era the local history tends to become confused.

Considering the margin of error possible in a work of this kind, Mrs. Rebekah Baines Johnson did a very meritorious and commendable job in *A Family Album,* particularly in establishing the many genealogical lines involved and gathering from many sources the pictures included in this volume. Moreover, Mrs. Johnson has provided many valuable insights into the character and qualities of the family membership in her biographical essays and sketches.

JOHN S. MOURSUND

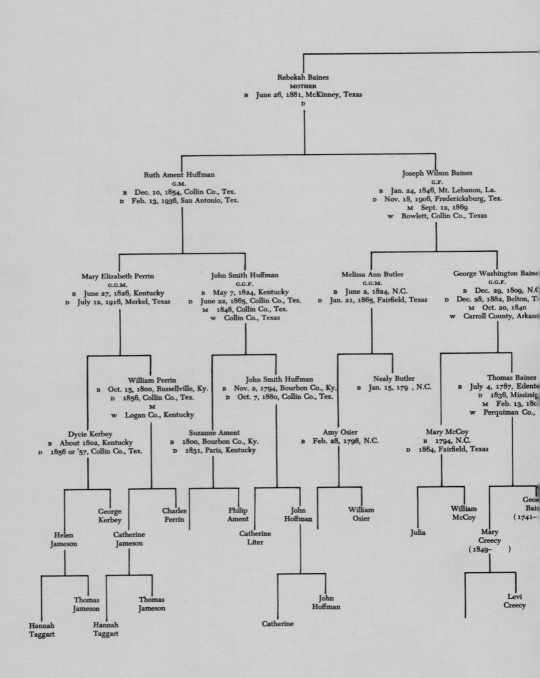

Rebekah Baines
MOTHER
B June 26, 1881, McKinney, Texas
D

Ruth Ament Huffman
G.M.
B Dec. 10, 1854, Collin Co., Tex.
D Feb. 13, 1936, San Antonio, Tex.

Joseph Wilson Baines
G.F.
B Jan. 24, 1846, Mt. Lebanon, La.
D Nov. 18, 1906, Fredericksburg, Tex.
M Sept. 12, 1869
W Rowlett, Collin Co., Texas

Mary Elizabeth Perrin
G.G.M.
B June 27, 1826, Kentucky
D July 12, 1916, Merkel, Texas

John Smith Huffman
G.G.F.
B May 7, 1824, Kentucky
D June 22, 1865, Collin Co., Tex.
M 1848, Collin Co., Tex.
W Collin Co., Texas

Melissa Ann Butler
G.G.M.
B June 2, 1824, N.C.
D Jan. 21, 1865, Fairfield, Texas

George Washington Baine
G.G.F.
B Dec. 29, 1809, N.C.
D Dec. 28, 1882, Belton, T
M Oct. 20, 1840
W Carroll County, Arkans

William Perrin
B Oct. 15, 1800, Russellville, Ky.
D 1856, Collin Co., Tex.
M
W Logan Co., Kentucky

John Smith Huffman
B Nov. 2, 1794, Bourbon Co., Ky.
D Oct. 7, 1880, Collin Co., Tex.

Nealy Butler
B Jan. 15, 179 , N.C.

Thomas Baines
B July 4, 1787, Edente
D 1836, Mississip
M Feb. 13, 180
W Perquiman Co.,

Dycie Kerbey
B About 1802, Kentucky
D 1856 or '57, Collin Co., Tex.

Suzanne Ament
B 1800, Bourbon Co., Ky.
D 1831, Paris, Kentucky

Amy Osier
B Feb. 28, 1796, N.C.

Mary McCoy
B 1794, N.C.
D 1864, Fairfield, Texas

Helen
Jameson

George
Kerbey

Catherine
Jameson

Charles
Perrin

Philip
Ament

John
Hoffman

William
Osier

William
McCoy

Geo
Bain
(1741–

Julia

Catherine
Liter

Mary
Creecy
(1849–)

Thomas
Jameson

Thomas
Jameson

Hannah
Taggart

Hannah
Taggart

John
Hoffman

Levi
Creecy

Catherine

THIS IS THE LINEAGE OF
Lyndon Baines Johnson
Johnson City, Texas

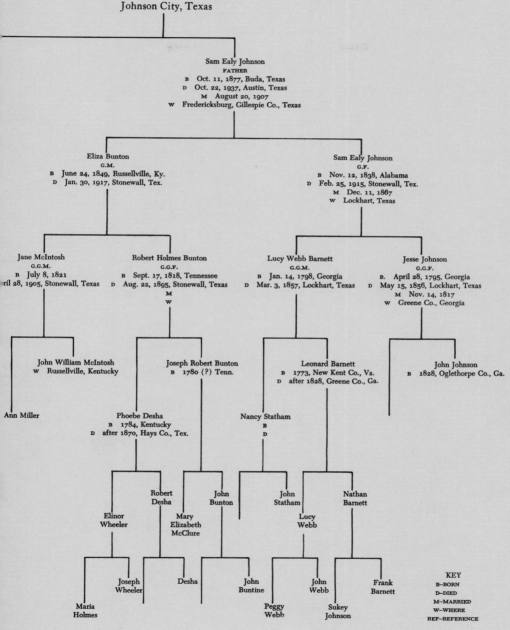

Sam Ealy Johnson
FATHER
B   Oct. 11, 1877, Buda, Texas
D   Oct. 22, 1937, Austin, Texas
M   August 20, 1907
W   Fredericksburg, Gillespie Co., Texas

Eliza Bunton
G.M.
B   June 24, 1849, Russellville, Ky.
D   Jan. 30, 1917, Stonewall, Tex.

Sam Ealy Johnson
G.F.
B   Nov. 12, 1838, Alabama
D   Feb. 25, 1915, Stonewall, Tex.
M   Dec. 11, 1867
W   Lockhart, Texas

Jane McIntosh
G.G.M.
B   July 8, 1821
ril 28, 1905, Stonewall, Texas

Robert Holmes Bunton
G.G.F.
B   Sept. 17, 1818, Tennessee
D   Aug. 22, 1895, Stonewall, Texas
M
W

Lucy Webb Barnett
G.G.M.
B   Jan. 14, 1798, Georgia
D   Mar. 3, 1857, Lockhart, Texas

Jesse Johnson
G.G.F.
B.   April 28, 1795, Georgia
D   May 15, 1856, Lockhart, Texas
M   Nov. 14, 1817
W   Greene Co., Georgia

John William McIntosh
W   Russellville, Kentucky

Joseph Robert Bunton
B   1780 (?) Tenn.

Leonard Barnett
B   1773, New Kent Co., Va.
D   after 1828, Greene Co., Ga.

John Johnson
B   1828, Oglethorpe Co., Ga.

Ann Miller

Phoebe Desha
B   1784, Kentucky
D   after 1870, Hays Co., Tex.

Nancy Statham
B
D

Robert
Desha

John
Bunton

John
Statham

Nathan
Barnett

Elinor
Wheeler

Mary
Elizabeth
McClure

Lucy
Webb

Joseph
Wheeler

Desha

John
Buntine

John
Webb

Frank
Barnett

Maria
Holmes

Peggy
Webb

Sukey
Johnson

KEY
B—BORN
D—DIED
M—MARRIED
W—WHERE
REF—REFERENCE

Lyndon Baines Johnson
and His Parents

Lyndon Baines Johnson

It was daybreak, Thursday, August 27, 1908, on the Sam Johnson farm on the Pedernales River near Stonewall, Gillespie County. In the rambling old farmhouse of the young Sam Johnsons, lamps had burned all night. Now the light came in from the east, bringing a deep stillness, a stillness so profound and so pervasive that it seemed as if the earth itself were listening. And then there came a sharp compelling cry —the most awesome, happiest sound known to human ears—the cry of a newborn baby; the first child of Sam Ealy and Rebekah Johnson was "discovering America".

He was a large, well-formed child weighing about ten pounds, the attending physician, Dr. John Blanton of Buda, estimated. His grandmother Baines was first to take him in her arms, calling him a wonderful boy, with which Aunt Kate Keele agreed, adding that she could see the Bunton favor.

The proud father—never was there a prouder—assured that all was well with his wife and son, dashed out of the house to saddle Fritz, his splendid grey horse, and gallop up the road to break the glad news, "It's a boy," to his parents in the next farmhouse and other kin farther up the road.

The birth of their son brought great happiness and great changes in the lives of the Sam Johnsons. The father had ardently desired a son and each day his plans and hopes for the boy grew. The mother looked into her son's brown eyes seeing in them not only the quick intelligence and fearless spirit that animated her husband's flashing eyes, but also the deep purposefulness and true nobility that had shone in her father's steady brown eyes. The boy brought new purpose and greater happiness to her life.

The baby, the first Baines grandchild but the fifth in the Johnson family, was a great favorite with all the kinfolk. He was bright and bonny, a happy, winsome child, who made friends easily, ate and slept as he should, and woke with a laugh instead of a wail. "Such a beautiful, such a wonderful baby", his mother thought early one November morning as she lay watching the baby in his crib beside her bed, and her indignation mounted, "no name yet". "Time to get breakfast, Rebekah; the room is warm", said Sam, lacing his boots by the crackling fire. Suddenly Rebekah spoke: "Sam, I'm not getting up to cook breakfast until this baby is named. He is nearly three months old and the most wonderful baby in the world and still called 'Baby'. I've submitted all the names I know and you always turn them down. Now you suggest and I'll pass judgment". Sam was usually the one who issued the ultimatums, but Rebekah's, occasional and surprising as they were, achieved results. "How do you like Clarence?" he asked. "Not one bit", came the quick answer, "try again". "Then what about Dayton?" came next. "Much better; but still not quite right for this boy", she replied. "What do you think about Linden for him?" Sam asked. "That's fine", was the considered reply, "if I may spell it as I like. Lin*den* isn't so euphonious as Lyn*don* Johnson would be". "Spell it as you please", her husband smiled, "he will still be named for my friend Linden. So now the boy is named Lyndon Baines Johnson. Come cook breakfast; the naming is over". She kissed the baby's rosy cheek and soon hurried to the kitchen to make the biscuits.

The first years of Lyndon's life sped swiftly. He was a very active and healthy child and was busy from sunrise to sundown. He loved the farm animals and his dog, "Bigham Young". He enjoyed running off to Grandpa Johnson's and eating "apples" from Grandpa's desk. Grandpa was very proud of this grandson, and predicted a great future for him, writing to his daughter Lucie out West, "I have a mighty fine grandson, smart as you find them. I expect him to be United States Senator before he is forty".

When he rested after lunch and before bedtime, he listened with avid interest and many questions to the stories his mother told him from the Bible, history, and myths especially the ones that really happened. She taught him the alphabet from blocks before he was two; all the Mother Goose rhymes and poems from Longfellow and Tennyson at three; and when he was four he could spell many words beginning with "Grandpa" down to "Dan", a favorite horse, and "cat", and could read. Always generous, he showered his mother with gifts, pebbles and flowers, "buying everything pretty in the magazines" for his mother.

When school at Junction opened, every recess found Lyndon over to play with Ava and Margaret and the other children so his mother persuaded the teacher, Miss Katie Deadrich, to take him as a pupil. Lyndon completed a primer and a reader, but his school term was cut short by whooping cough.

The next year the Johnsons moved to Johnson City where he began the first grade under Miss Florence Walker. He and Kittie Clyde Ross were leaders of their class and spoke at the closing of school. Lyndon delivered a poem of his own selection, "I'd Rather Be Mamma's Boy".

After several years in Johnson City, the family went back to the farm at Stonewall. It was at this time that his parents were pleased to note the development, initiative and resourcefulness in the boy. He had a passion for truthfulness and could be depended on to admit a failure in duty or obedience. His mother was shocked and indignant when a kinsman declared "All children tell stories", and she retorted: "My boy never tells a lie".

He liked the farm and rode to school a few miles away on his pony. He had a group of boy friends all older than he and usually brought one home to spend the night.

In 1923 the family returned to their home in Johnson City so that Lyndon might complete his Senior year in school. He graduated from high school in May 1924. He was the president of his class of six. He and Johnnie Brooks Casparis won the debate in the Blanco County Interscholastic League.

He had led the normal uneventful, but enjoyable life, of a popular, fun-loving teen-ager. The Redford and Crider boys were his closest pals and one, or more, of them was usually spending the night with him. Now followed a period of indecision and indifference. His parents were eager for him to attend college, but his mild interest in books at this time was discouraging. He had his first job at Robstown. He was restless and embarked with the Crider and Summy boys on an expedition to California. This experience of a few months proved a test of the boy in many ways and helped to clarify his ideas. He came home and drove a tractor on the highway for some months. This was hard, monotonous work, and his parents felt that he was wasting time and talents which should have been employed in school. His mother with characteristic persistence pressed home the fact that work is honorable whether with the hands or the head, but that education gives opportunity in every way. One raw cold afternoon, Lyndon came in from a particularly unpleasant day on the highway and announced, "I'm sick of working just with my hands and I'm ready to try working with my brain. Mother, if you and Daddy will get me in college, I'll go as soon as I can." His mother walked over to the phone and called San Marcos Teachers' College to inquire when the next semester opened. In February 1927, Lyndon entered college in San Marcos. In August 1930, he received his degree there, having completed during this period three months of subcollege work, four years of college, and one year of teaching at Cotulla. His grades were excellent, and he was a leader in many extracurricular activities and class administration. He worked in the office of the president of the college and edited the school paper. Inertia and indecision were in the past.

The next year he taught public speaking in Sam Houston High School in Houston. His debating team went to the State having won the District championship. He loved teaching and was popular with faculty and students.

In the fall of 1931, he resigned his position in the Houston schools to become Secretary to Congressman R. M. Kleberg. In making this change from teaching to political life, he was aided and abetted by his father, whose overwhelming ambition for his son was governmental position. The wisdom of his judgment of Lyndon's ability and aptitude for service in this field has been justified by Lyndon's advancement and success.

Sam Ealy Johnson, Jr.

Sam Ealy Johnson, Jr., fifth child and first son of Sam Ealy and Eliza (Bunton) Johnson, was born October 11, 1877 at Buda, Hays County, Texas. The arrival of a son brought great joy to the Johnson household, as Sam Johnson had longed for a son and, despite his great pride in "the four prettiest little girls in ten counties", had strongly resented the banter of his friends who jokingly called him "Gal Johnson". Eliza, too, looked with great tenderness on this child whose dark eyes, black curls and white skin were a Bunton inheritance and whose mental alertness and traits of leadership could be traced back to her beloved Deshas. So the precocious, attractive boy, Sam, was the darling of the home. Attired as nearly as possible like his father, he accompanied him whenever possible, and at an early age acquired an unusual poise and assurance. He had a quick mind, keen perception, and an amazing memory. An elder sister memorizing a poem of thirty-two verses for recital the last day of school was astounded to hear the child, Sam, far below school age recite it in its entirety. He was extremely active and loved all sports. When he was about eleven, the Johnsons moved to Gillespie County locating on the Pedernales River near Stonewall. The tasks and delights of farm life presented a challenge to Sam; he must ride faster; plow longer, straighter rows; pick more cotton than his companions. This sense of competition was a strong urge through out his life.

He was ambitious and longed for an education. His services on the farm were needed and it required sacrifice on the part of his parents much of the time to send him to school at nearby Johnson City. Once his father gave him some cattle saying, "This is all I can do on your schooling this year." Each weekend the young high school student turned butcher, slaughtered and cut up a steer and sold steaks and soupbones to tide him over until next "butchering day". Later on, he bought a barber's chair and tools from the town barber, who had become ill and had to give up his work. Soon Sam was a full-fledged barber on Saturdays and afternoons after school. His ingenuity in devising jobs to keep him in school was unavailing however, when he became a victim of indigestion. He was forced to leave school and his parents sent him out to West Texas hoping that on the ranch of his uncle, Lucius Bunton, he might regain his health.

After a few months in Marfa, he came home, determined to teach school. With thirteen books, the required subjects for examination for a teacher's certificate, a bottle of pepsin tablets and a sack of dried fruit, (doctor's recommendation) he sought out Grandmother Bunton and laid his problem before her. Grandmother was very fond of "Sammie" and was glad to cooperate by taking him into her quiet little home, a great contrast to the lively Johnson home where the other eight sons and daughters were either still living at home or dropping in for visits. After a few weeks of study, Sam took the teachers' examination and obtained the coveted certificate. In later years he often recalled with pleasure that he made 100% in both Texas and United States history; he always loved history and government.

In the fall of 1896, he opened school at White Oak School at Sandy in a one-room schoolhouse with pupils of all sizes and ages, some older and larger than he. It was his purpose to teach and if the student's capacities proved limited, the young schoolteacher's methods varied accordingly. Each was to him an individual problem. He boarded with Mr. and Mrs. Young, and Mrs. Young liked to tell of his youthful dignity, pleasing manners, and his playing with the baby.

The next year he taught the Rocky School near Hye. He boarded with the Shipp family, and around the fire in the evening listened with great interest to the experience of Captain Rufus Perry, the Indian fighter.

He wanted to study law—he had the type of mind for it and he loved law—but found it necessary to make a living immediately so he decided to rent his father's land and move to "the old house", the first farm home of his parents. For several years he and his farm hands operated the Johnson farm with considerable success, hard work and great enjoyment. Travelers timed their trips "to make it to little Sam Johnson's by nightfall in order to spend the night and enjoy a good time". (Incidentally "little Sam" was six feet, but the adjective was used to distinguish him from his father, "big Sam".) His most frequent visitors were three friends and boon companions: W. C. Linden and Dayton Moses, lawyers of Statewide repute and Kay Alexander, teacher and engineer, all brilliant and able men.

In 1904, he was elected to the State legislature from the 89th District. At this time he was a personable young man, slender and graceful, immaculately groomed, agreeable and affable in manner and with great personal magnetism. He was happy and interested in his work. He felt keenly and understood with clarity the needs of his State, and worked conscientiously and effectively on beneficial and needed legislation. This was the beginning of nearly twelve years of service in the 29th, 30th, 35th, 36th, 37th, and 38th legislatures.

He was the author of the Alamo Purchase Bill, a bill appropriating $3,000,000 to help the drouth-stricken of West Texas, a bill providing for the erection of a home for the widows of Confederate soldiers, the Johnson Blue Sky Law, and many other constructive legislative measures. He was famous for his speech on tolerance delivered on the floor of the House during World War I, in which he stressed patriotism tempered with common sense and justice. He was also a leader in the first rural relief program for Texas during the drouth of 1917–1918 and did much for the improvement of our highways.

His association with the leading statesmen and political figures of the day was stimulating and deeply gratifying to Sam. He was a conscientious, unselfish and farsighted public servant. He was always sympathetic to the needs of the poor, the unfortunate, the deserving, and was active in giving of his time and service. He secured pensions for many Confederate soldiers and widows and Texas rangers and through his efforts a Congressional amendment was passed, granting pensions to four hundred Texas rangers who served during the Civil War period. Often hearing of a Confederate soldier or a Ranger who merited a pension, he would seek out the man and talk over his record with him; then leave no stone unturned until he had secured his pension.

In August 1907, after a whirlwind courtship of a few months he married Rebekah Baines, the daughter of his predecessor in the legislature. In disposition, upbringing and background, these two were vastly dissimilar. However, in principles and motives, the real essentials of life, they were one. Their marriage of thirty years broken only by death was based on mutual trust, respect and love. The chief desire of both was to give their five children a happy comfortable home, the assurance of the interest and love of their parents, the best advantages within their reach, and good educations. Life was often complex and strenuous, but it was full of satisfying constructive work, fond hopes and ambitions and unity of purpose.

Sam Johnson had a great optimism which was dealt a severe blow when the San Francisco earthquake of 1906 wiped out his cotton holdings and saddled him with a debt of several thousand dollars. In the effort to supplement his finances, he bought and sold cotton with success until this unexpected loss occurred. He was an excellent farmer, a good judge of cattle which he bought and drove to market, a splendid trader and withal industrious, farsighted, keen in judgment. He had a great love for the land, and enjoyed farming very much.

For some years, he was engaged in the real estate business dealing principally with farms and ranches. He established an enviable record of satisfying both the seller and the buyer in every transaction. He was able to see both sides and dealt fairly and honestly with all.

In 1930, he accepted a position as Inspector for the Motor Bus Division of the Railroad Commission, who spoke of him in this wise: "Sam Johnson's diplomacy, knowledge of conditions throughout the State, his tact in dealing with men, his sound judgment, untiring energy and agreeable personality render him especially qualified for this position.

He had heard and adjusted many difficulties arising from the enforcement of these laws".

After spending almost four years in San Marcos in order to place his five children in college, he and his wife returned to their home in Johnson City in the fall of 1934. He was happy to get back to the town where the greater part of his life had been spent and enjoyed making improvements on the house, setting out an orchard, tending a vegetable garden and planting flowers in the yard. He was a natural farmer and his crops and garden flourished, but for the first time in his life, he had time to devote to the beautifying of the yard, and the results of his work there were most rewarding in flowers of exceptional beauty, size and profusion.

It was found that he had a serious heart affliction and a very grave illness in 1935 was followed by the restriction of his activities. To one who had lived so strenuously and so richly, this was indeed a great cross. He was reluctant to accept his physical limitations and bravely tried to continue his work. Another severe heart attack took place in the summer of 1937, followed by a long and painful illness. After a stay in the hospital, he rallied sufficiently to be taken to the home of his son, Lyndon, in Austin where after two weeks he passed away October 23, 1937. On Sunday he was laid to rest in the family graveyard near Stonewall. Three friends, Lon Smith, N. T. Stubbs and Rev. J. H. Clark, paid tribute to the man they loved and honored.

He was ambitious not so much for his own success as for that of his friends and his children, being alert to the interests of a loved one and persistent in his promotion of the same. In his own advancement, he was retiring and modest.

He had a fine sense of organization and always thought out carefully the problems confronting him in the fields of his varied activities, determining the desired solution, or goal, and then devising with ingenuity and ability the best and most economical means for acquiring the desired result. He always completely mastered a line of work before undertaking it.

His judgment of men was almost infalliable, and his decision regarding issues and underlying motives was discerning and acute.

He had a sound and sage philosophy which he expressed by a quoted axiom, proverb or Scriptural passage. He liked to illustrate a situation by relating a remembered incident in history, a humorous anecdote, or a personal experience. He was an interesting conversationalist with a broad knowledge of State and national affairs, political figures and issues, and a deep understanding of people, their ideas, capacities, and desires. He delighted in being of service to those in need, giving sympathy and practical aid freely. Small wonder that "The House by the Side of the Road" was a favorite of his, as he was truly "a friend to man", extending hospitality to the truck driver who broke down in front of his door as graciously as to the Governor of the State who dropped in to talk politics.

Highly organized, sensitive, and nervous, he was impatient of inefficiency and ineptitude and quick to voice his displeasure; equally quick, however, in making amends when some word of his caused pain to another. He was the most forgiving of men when an injury had been done to him, making excuses for the offender and completely forgetting the offense.

He was intensely loyal and generous far beyond his means. His faith in a real and personal Heavenly Father was strong. To those who knew him best, great-heart seems best to describe him.

As his friend Lon Smith said beside his grave,

> "He was a man
> Take him for all and all,
> I shall not look upon his like again."

Rebekah Baines

Viewing my life in retrospect, I am inclined to borrow from Bing Crosby's biography its title, "Call Me Lucky", for in the circumstances and associations of my life I have indeed been most fortunate.

In my birth, June 26, 1881 at McKinney, Texas, I was fortunate in being the first-born of my parents, a happy circumstance of superior advantage. Again my choice of parents was most felicitous; they were a happy, well-adjusted, and devoted couple who welcomed me into a well-ordered, peaceful home to which cross words and angry looks were foreign.

At an incredibly early age, my father taught me to read; reading has been one of the great pleasures and sustaining forces of my life. He taught me how to study, to think and to endure, the principles of mathematics, the beauty of simple things. He taught me that "a lie is an abomination to the Lord" and to all real people the world over; he taught me obedience and self-control, saying that without them no one is worthy of responsibility or trust. He gave the timid child self-confidence.

My mother was the cheeriest, most energetic, and serenest of persons. She was hospitable and friendly, resourceful and ingenious. She had great sanity, sweetness, and purity.

I am grateful for the little town of Blanco, my excellent teachers, men of ability and education not often found in such small places, my Baptist upbringing, sermons, prayer meeting and Sunday School; the splendid young people who were my companions and classmates—the

Alexanders, Bells, Capts, Edwardses, Brighams, and Stubbses, many of them have gone far in the world; and all the neighborliness, the delights, the chores, and the charms of that simple, friendly, dearly loved town, Blanco. I love to think of our home, a two-story rock house with a fruitful orchard of perfectly spaced trees, terraced flower beds, broad walks, purple plumed wisteria climbing to the room, fragrant honeysuckle at the dining room windows whose broad sills were seats for us children. Most of all I love to think of the gracious hospitality of that home, of the love and trust, the fear of God, and the beautiful ideals that made it a true home.

In the early 1900's, my father suffered severe and sudden financial reverses. I am glad to say that we adjusted readily and cheerfully to the financial change. My brother sold his horse and rubber-tired buggy and returned to A and M College where he worked to defray his expenses until he received his degree. I took charge of the College book store at Baylor College to pay my expenses for my final year there. My father, however, grieved over his inability to continue his generous provision for his family and his health became greatly impaired. He sought a new location for his legal practice and moved to Fredericksburg in 1904. After a lingering illness, he passed away November 18, 1906; so was broken our family circle. This was the first sorrow of my life and it required all my determination and strength of will to adjust myself to life without my father, who had been the dominant force in my life as well as my adored parent, reverenced mentor, and most interesting companion.

We moved into the little home which my father had designed and had built and which had engaged his last loving thoughts of provision for his family. I continued teaching Expression classes and corresponding for daily newspapers. Fredericksburg might have been transplanted from the old world, its customs, ideas, and pursuits were unique and foreign; the people were thrifty, clean, hard-working, honest and self-respecting; most of all they were kind, and their friendliness warmed our lonely saddened hearts. Mrs. Oscar Krauskopf and Mr. Alfred Vander Stucken will be remembered with gratitude all my days. I presented plays with the help of the music teacher, Miss Ophelia Brown. I had a small congenial circle of friends, Julia Estill, Elsbeth and Frank Hanisch, Lorlie Wahrmund, Charlie Darrogh, Emil Sauer, Alfred Brodie, and Dr. Peden and his sister, Ada. The quiet unexciting associations of this period were enlivened by frequent visits from a dashing and dynamic young legislator, Sam Johnson. He took me to the Confederate Reunion where we enjoyed the oratory of Senators Joe Bailey and Charlie Culberson and Governor Tom Campbell. With his sister, Lucie, and brother, George, we heard William Jennings Bryan, whom we both admired extravagantly, address the Legislature. He was enchanted to find a girl who really liked politics. We were married August 20, 1907 and moved out to the farm on the Pedernales River in Gillespie County where we farmed between legislative sessions. And so began a new life for me.

Normally the first year of marriage is a period of readjustment. In this case, I was confronted not only by the problem of adjustment to a completely opposite personality, but also to a strange and new way of life, a way far removed from that I had known in Blanco and Fredericksburg. Recently my early experiences on the farm were relived when I saw "The Egg and I"; again I shuddered over the chickens, and wrestled with a mammoth iron stove. However, I was determined to overcome circumstances instead of letting them overwhelm me. At last I realized that life is real and earnest and not the charming fairy tale of which I had so long dreamed. This was the beginning of thirty years of married life, thirty busy beautiful years engaged in making a living and rearing five wonderful children who consumed our energies, our hopes and plans. In the essentials of life Sam and I were agreed, but we had definite and opposing ideas on many lesser things, which makes for interest and piquancy in life. We went to San Marcos in 1930 to put the children in college and that completed, returned to our home in Johnson City to grow old together, quietly and happily, improving our home, enjoying visits from our children and doing all the things the rushing pace of the past had precluded. But this happiness was short-lived. Sam developed a serious heart ailment, a condition which caused him agonized suffering until death brought relief in October 1937. It was hard to believe that the brilliant mind, the dynamic personality, the great and loving heart of Sam Johnson were forever stilled. It is hard to undo the clasp of the hand that has held yours through all the trials and triumphs of thirty years. I grieve that he never lived to see the bright faces of the precious grandchildren who delight my heart; that he cannot be here to see the accomplishments of Lyndon in governmental affairs, which Sam so loved, and the national leadership our son has won; that he cannot smile with me over the characteristics he passed on to Sam Houston, political insight and prediction, sensitivity and pride, his bearing and figure; that he cannot rejoice in the fact that his beautiful daughters are all happily married to fine men and each has a promising child. But it was not God's will.

The "old order changeth" and the tempo of life is slower now. Once there was never time enough to do all I wanted to do; now I must devise plans to prevent my slipping into the "stark sloth and arrant ease" of old age. I engage my thoughts and energies in compiling family histories which I hope may be of interest, help, and inspiration to my children. I indulge my love for the beautiful in collecting American pressed glass; each sparkling goblet holds interest and beauty. There is time now for the house and I enjoy its comforts and conveniences, the furniture which was my mother's, my antiques, keepsakes and pictures. To be in my own home means a great deal to me, and I am grateful for the generosity and thoughtfulness that provided this for me. Here I have my books so beloved through all my days now more needed than ever before. I enjoy the television that brings the news of the world, drama, instruction and entertainment to me. Chief of those pleasures is the sight of my son as he goes about his work in the nation's capital

I find greatest happiness in my children, their visits and attentions, their love and interest, the mates they have chosen who have become so dear to me because of their devotion to my children and their consideration and affection for me. I relive my life with my children in my grandchildren. Of course my sweet Lynda Bird is a personality in her own right but in her sparkling brown eyes, her affectionate manner, her brilliant mind, her persistence, her sympathetic nature, her indomitable will, I see Lyndon. She says "I love you so Maday" and I hear also in boyish accents, "I love my mamma best in the world." In my demure Lucy Baines, I like to trace the Baines characteristics of self-sufficiency, poise, reserve, inner resourcefulness, and independence. Of course they both also inherit many traits from their wonderful mother, who has countless highly admirable traits.

I cannot say with Browning that old age is "the best of life", for the years of accomplishment and productivity, of struggle and activity to me make the best period of life, but in recounting my many blessings I say again I am most fortunate.

My favorite quotation from the great philosopher and poet, Browning, is one which for many years has deeply influenced my life,
"The common problem, yours and mine, everyone's,/Is not to fancy what were fair in life/Provided it could be—but finding first/What may be and how to make it fair up to our means."

Lyndon's first picture. He was six months old.

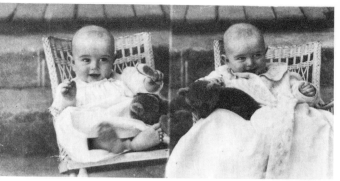

When Sam was returning from the home of the neighbor who took this picture, he raised his hand holding the package as he saw me waiting on the porch and began to run I ran to meet him and we met in the middle of the Benner pasture to exclaim rapturously over the photograph of our boy. We had never seen a picture more beautiful nor did we ever!

Aunt Lucie took this picture in the walk at Grandpa Johnson's place.

At eighteen months.

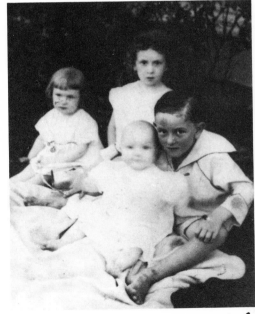

*Notice Lyndon's protective air: he
was very fond of his little brother.*

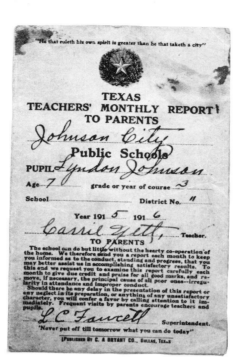

"He that ruleth his own spirit is greater than he that taketh a city"

TEXAS
TEACHERS' MONTHLY REPORT
TO PARENTS

Johnson City

Public Schools

PUPIL *Lyndon Johnson*

Age *7*   grade or year of course *3*

School _____   District No. *11*

Year 191 *5*   191 *6*

Carrie Yett, Teacher.

TO PARENTS

The school can do but little without the hearty co-operation of the home. We therefore send you a report each month to keep you informed as to the conduct, standing and progress, that you may better assist us in accomplishing satisfactory results. To this end we request you to examine this report carefully each month to give due credit and praise for all good marks, and remove, if necessary, the principal cause of all poor ones—irregularity in attendance and improper conduct.

Should there be any delay in the presentation of this report or any neglect in its preparation, or anything of any unsatisfactory character, you will confer a favor by calling attention to it immediately. Frequent visits by parents encourage teachers and pupils.

L C Fawcett Superintendent.

"Never put off till tomorrow what you can do today"

[PUBLISHED BY C. A BRYANT CO., DALLAS, TEX.S]

Up at Grandpa Johnson's on Sunday.

Lyndon was about
four and had golden
curls at this time

In a pensive mood.

TEXAS
TEACHERS' MONTHLY REPORT
TO PARENTS

Johnson City

Public Schools

PUPIL *Lyndon Johnson*

Age *8* grade or year of course *Fourth*

School_____ District No._____

Year 191*6* 191*7*

Zeta Bradley, Teacher.

TO PARENTS

The school can do but little without the hearty co-operation of the home. We therefore send you a report each month to keep you informed as to the conduct, standing and progress, that you may better assist us in accomplishing satisfactory results. To this end we request you to examine this report carefully each month to give due credit and praise for all good marks, and remove, if necessary, the principal cause of all poor ones—irregularity in attendance and improper conduct.

Should there be any delay in the presentation of this report or any neglect in its preparation, or anything of any unsatisfactory character, you will confer a favor by calling attention to it immediately. Frequent visits by parents encourage teachers and pupils.

_____ Superintendent

Never put off till tomorrow what you can do today

Published By C. A. Bryan Co., Dallas, Texas

Up at Uncle Toms
playing with his
Cousins and Kittie Clyde.

Christmas at
Uncle Clarences

Lyndon and Mamie in the first years of high school.

At Stonewall in 1921. Lyndon brought home the photographer and arranged this grouping. He is wearing his first long trousers.

In 1924

This class is on dep't basis and I
am the sponsor. See Red...

Lyndon's First School

This was made shortly before Lyndon's graduation from Johnson City High School. His classmates were Margaret Johnson, Kittie Clyde Ross, Georgia Cammack Louise Casparis and John Dollahite.

Lyndon and Lorene.

In California.

Christmas 1926.

Class officers have been elect-
at the Southwest Texas State
Teachers College, San Marcos, as
follows:
President, senior class, Albert
Hartzke of Giddings, right, above;
Lyndon Johnson of Johnson City,
right, below, senior legislator; Day
Brandt of Lamkin, left, above,
junior class president; Frank Arnold of San Marcos, left, below,
junior legislator.

4-17-1930

To Our Mothers

(By Lyndon Johnson)

*Calvin Coolidge, in writing of his life says: "It
ems impossible that any man could adequately de-
ribe his mother. I cannot describe mine. We laid
other away in the blustering snows of March. The
eatest grief that can come to a boy came to me.
fe was never to seem the same again".*

*Those words re-echo in human hearts the world
er. Where can there be found words to describe
e's mother? What adjectives can portray her in-
ite patience, her unfailing tenderness, her loving
re, her amazing self-sacrifice, her wonderful un-
rstanding, her intense loyalty? All vocabularies
il when we attempt to describe Mother's traits, but
are most appalled with the emptiness of the lang-
ge when we contemplate the love of mother.*

*The affection of friends, sweethearts, brothers,
ters, of all loved ones may be estranged but moth-
's love abides to the end. Disaster, disgrace, des-
ir and death do not affect the love a mother feels
r her child save to add to it compassion and ten-
rness. There is no love on earth comparable to
at of mother. Our best description of it is that of
types of earthly love, it most nearly approaches
divine.*

*Every heart gives a throb of sympathy in re-
onse to Coolidge's words descriptive of the loss of
mother. How true, agonizingly true, it is that the
eatest grief that can come to a child is the loss of
mother. Life, truly is never the same again.*

*We know all this. Our minds acknowledge the
eat debt mankind owes to mothers. Our hearts de-
re its truth. Let us today make our lives living
butes and fitting memorials to the splendid char-
ters who have proven the most potent and vital
rce for good in the world—the mothers of men.*

ON CHRONICLE

CHOSEN AT SAN MARCOS COLLEGE

LYNDON B. JOHNSON
Johnson City
B. S.; History.
B. A. Club, Press Club, Student
Council, Harris Blair, College
Star, Pi Gamma Mu.

SENIORS

During Lyndons college years, he wrote home:
"Mother, I am now learning the things
you have been trying to teach me since
I was a little boy."
He loved his home very dearly and
came home every possible week-end and
wrote his mother almost every day.

The PEDAGOG 1930

Schoolmaster's Club

LYNDON JOHNSON, *Secretary*

A. C. HASTINGS — *President*
F. S. HERRON — *Vice-President*
LYNDON JOHNSON — *Secretary*

The Schoolmaster's Club is an organization sponsored by the College for the social and educational benefit of its men students and faculty members.

The peak of the Club's social season was reached in a watermelon feast held at Wimberley during the summer session.

Debate

In 1927-'28 four teams, coached by M. L. Arnold and H. M. Greene, were placed in the field, bringing credit to themselves and to the college. The first debate was with Abilene Christian College at San Marcos, in which G. Preston Smith and Frank Jordan, of S. W. T. T. C., were defeated by a two to one decision in favor of the A. C. C. team which had already debated the question several times. This defeat, however, was completely erased in a debate later, on the same question, with Howard Payne, in which the local team defeated the Yellow Jackets, who had previously defeated the A. C. C. parliamentarians in a three to nothing decision. Hence, victory over Howard Payne morally amounted to victory over A. C. C.

Elmer Graham and Lyndon Johnson journeyed over to Huntsville and brought home the long end of a two to one decision. The fourth debate of the season was held at San Marcos with McMurry College. Again the local team, Alfred Schmid and Richard Spinn, was pitted against a team that was experienced in the question. The decision was two to one in favor of the visitors. Another debate was scheduled with Canyon, the T. I. A. A. rival. Tellie LaBauve and Clarence Boatright, representing the college, were the only ones to defend the affirmative the question for the year: "Resolved, that the U. S. should cease to protect, by armed force, capital invested in foreign countries."

Top Row: Boatright, Graham, Johnson
Bottom Row: LaBauve, Schmid, Spinn, Williams

Boody and Lyndon

Press Club

LYNDON JOHNSON, *President*

OFFICERS

LYNDON JOHNSON	President
HELEN HOFHEINZ	Secretary

The Press Club was organized in the fall of 1925 for the purpose of fostering and stimulating a higher type of college journalism. A student is eligible to membership in the club who has made at least ten grade points in each of the two terms prior to his election, who has demonstrated exceptional literary ability, who has edited or been business manager of either of the student publications, who has served two terms on either of the staffs of the student publications, or who has won any of the individual events in the local elimination contest for the Texas Intercollegiate Press Association contest.

Lyndon Johnson, President of the Press Club, was the club's delegate to the annual T. I. P. A. convention at Huntsville.

Top row: DEASON, DEZELLE, HOFHEINZ, HYDE, FRAZER.
Bottom row: LANE, McKINNEY, TOM NICHOLS, RICHARDS, SORELLE, H. E. SPECK.

Southwest Texas Teachers College.

tries to improve himself and
es not know what real happi-

If men should rise from the dead
epitaphs, many would think they
wrong grave.—John Flavel.

BLISHED BY THE STUDENTS OF SAM HOUSTON STATE TEACHERS COLLEGE, HUNTSVILLE, TEXAS, APRIL 25, 1928

"PRINC
MAY 1

SAM HOUSTON DE-BATERS WIN FROM HOWARD PAYNE

ORD=COU

THE RECORD-COURIER

April 26, 1928

on City, Texas, October 18, 1928

JOHNSON-GRAHAM WIN

The Bearkat forensic men came through with colors flying high for the first time of the year Monday night in the auditorium when they won a two to one decision over Howard Payne College.

Arthur Hayes and Dewitt Chadick in their second debate within a week's time had a hard fighting team on their hands but came back n their two minute rejoinder to save the day. The debate was the most tightly contested to be held in Huntsville this year with both sides of the question being well represented.

The Sam Houston men defended the affirmative side of the question; "Resolved that the United States should cease protecting capital invested in foreign countries, except after formal declaration of war." Jesse Fox, Alcalde editor served as chairman.

San Marcos won the annual inter-collegiate debate from Sam Houston by a 2 to 1 decision last Thursday night.

Dewitt Chaddick and Arthur Hayes, as represenatives for S. H. S. T. C, could not prove that the United States shou'd cease to protect her capital in reign countries except after a formal declaration of war.

The outstanding feature of he debate was the last speech f the evening made by Johnson f San Marcos when he destroy-Houston's chance for his five minute re-

—o—

Lyndon B. Johnson

It always affords us pleasure to make mention of any of Blanco County boy or girl who "makes good" away from home. We feel that the subject of our sketch is deserving of special mention, and therefore the small bunch of flowers strewn here is a reward of merit won by the personal effort of a deserving young man.

Lyndon B. Johnson is a son of Mr. and Mrs. S. E. Johnson of this City. He was born and raised here, and received his early education in the Johnson City High School, and is a graduate of the Class of 1924. After completing his studies here, Lyndon entered the Southwest Texas Teachers College at San Marcos, where he remained for two years. During this time he was employed in the office of President Evans of that institu-

While at College, Lyndon was selected to represent his class on the Student Welfare Council. He was on the debating team that won a decisive victory over the Sam Houston Teachers College at Huntsville, and the only Sophomore to ever be elected editor of The College Star, the student paper at S. W. T. T. C. He was also selected to conduct the "bigger and better athletic drive," and won distinction in this capacity.

Lyndon has always taken a great interest in literary and press club work and was one of the Texas Press reporters to attend the Democratic National Convention in Houston, and won distinction among the press boys who represented the largest papers in the United States.

At present Lyndon is principal of a ward school at Cotulla, and, judging from his past record, we are sure that he will make good. He has many friends at home who rejoice in his success, and wish him well in all his future undertakings.

Lyndon B. Johnson, son of Mr. and Mrs. S. E. Johnson of this city, and Elmer Graham of San Antonio representing the Southwest Texas Teachers College of San Marcos, defeated the Sam Houston State Teachers College team at Huntsville, on the 19th inst. in a debating contest of statewide importance. The negative side of the question, "Resolved, that the United States should cease to protect by armed forces, capital invested in foreign countries except after formal declaration of war," was sustained by Johnson and Graham. Young Johnson was first speaker on his side and had the last rejoiner.

Lyndon has made an excellent record in college for the past two terms, and has been prominently identified with many college activities. He is a member of the student Welfare Council, associate editor of the Pedagogue, the S. W. T. T. C. Annual, student manager of the Evans Field Drive editorial writer of The College Star, and was editor in chief of Freshman Edition of this publication last term. He is now a sophomore and his many friends here wish him continued success.

Lyndon Baines Johnson

It was with mixed emotions that we learned of the appointment of our able instructor, Lyndon Baines Johnson, as secretary to Representative Kleberg. Our first thought was the realization that he would no longer be with us, and that we would miss his friendship and guidance in the class room.

With that thought, however, came the realization that this meant promotion to him—that this was doubtless only the first step, politically, in a life of public service and that our loss would be another's gain.

As we pass along life's highway, we meet and mingle with those who seem destined to fill the higher positions of trust. Even though he enters a greater field of service, he has left with the student body those things which are monuments to his endeavors.

Students and faculty of Sam Houston will await with expectations future reports of Mr. Johnson in the halls of government at Washington.

MAY 1, 1932

Lyndon B. Johnson of San Marcos Named Head of Little Conference

Lyndon B. Johnson, secretary to Congressman Richard M. Kleberg of Kingsville, has been elected speaker of Little Congress, news dispatches from Washington state.

Johnson is the third Texan to hold the post in the past five years.

The Washington report characterizes his election as "unique," in that it has been the practice in the past to elevate subordinate officers in their regular order. Johnson, who has never held an office, was elected after a bitter fight.

Johnso is the son of Mr. and Mrs. S. E. Johnson of San Marcos. He attended San Marcos Teachers college, being closely associated with the administration, serving as a secretary.

EVERYTHING O.K. NOW

INTERNATIONAL NEWSREEL

The "Little Congress," an organization made up of secretaries to members of congress, is ready to operate now, since John Garner presented gavel, made from tree planted by General Sam Houston, to Lyndon B. Johnson, secretary to Representative Kleberg of Texas. Johnson is newly elected speaker of "Little Congress."

Who's Who In Sam Houston

LYNDON B. JOHNSON

Pleasing in personality, indefatigable in his labors, zealous in all of his undertakings. Although one of our newest faculty members, he has carved for himself a place in Sam Houston as one of the outstanding teachers.

Lyndon B. Johnson

JOHNSON LEAVES FOR WASHINGTON

Debate Instructor to Be Secretary To Congressman

Lyndon B. Johnson, former public speaking instructor at Sam Houston High School, has been selected as secretary to Richard M. Kleberg, newly elected congressman from Texas. Mr. Johnson was chosen for the position immediately after the election which filled the vacancy caused by the death of the late Representative Wurzbach.

Mr. Johnson worked his way through the San Marcos State Teachers College as secretary to President Evans of that institution.

He took charge of the public speaking class of Sam Houston in the fall of 1930, immediately after his graduation. During his brief period of work with the Sam Houston students, he turned out the debating team which lacked but one vote of winning the state championship in the finals at Austin last May.

"Mr. Johnson proved his ability as a teacher, as a debate coach, and as an inspired leader of youth," Principal W. J. Moyes stated Friday. "Students and faculty appreciate what he did for Sam Houston High while he was here, and expect to hear of many worthwhile accomplishments of Mr. Johnson in the field of politics which he is now entering."

TOWN TALK

It's His Job to Work Himself Out of a Job

By C. E. G.

It's his job to work himself out of a job.

The better he does his work, the sooner he will have to go to the rack, pull on his coat, straighten his tie and his chin and say, "Well folks, the fight's over. I'll be seeing you later."

Within a year's time, he has reduced his work about 33 1-3 per cent. Within that time he has seen kids pulled from the pool halls, the drug store corners, delivery trucks, and placed in position where they are educated to giving the country the benefits of that education.

His name is Lyndon Johnson. He is state director of the National Youth administration in Texas. He got his training in the hill country around Johnson City. He chopped weeds, cut grass. Decided he would get an education and did.

That was before rugged individualism became a by-word with people who really didn't care for rugged individualism except as an excuse to abuse the privileges which had been the heritage of this country.

"Sure," says Dir. Johnson, propping his feet on the desk and grinning broadly. "I guess I know a little bit about the youth's hard lot in life. You don't mind if I relax, do you."

I didn't. In fact, a man talks much better when he does relax. Then he told me how he started out.

"Received my early education in a country school in the Hill country. After schoolin', I got a job as a day laborer on the highways. I chopped weeds, earned a dollar here and a dollar there, always with an idea in my mind of finishing a college education."

It was this same desire which put Lyndon Johnson into college. He worked and studied at San Marcos. He learned how it felt to come home at night dog tired, turn on the lights, and try to whip a tired body into shape to absorb some mental training.

Later he went to Pearsall, then to Houston.

At Houston, he taught public speaking.

"There was a kid there named Gene Latimer. When he wasn't running around with the drug store gang, or delivering parcels, he was practicing debating. He had a knack at debating. I left for Washington. He left for South Texas and started driving a truck. I kept hearing from him. He wanted to go to school. So I brought him to Washington.

Now young Latimer is standing on his own two legs and is doing a good job with the government.

Out at the University of Texas law school there is another fellow who began picking up his education by studying at night, working by day. His name is L. E. Jones and he gets his law degree this year.

"Young Jones has already had several offers to go into a law office. He isn't, though, until he gets a degree. He used to deliver packages on a bicycle. He never could get away from the idea that he wanted an education. It came hard. He had a tough time. But he got the education. He is going places.

to the reds and other malcontents who seized such opportunities to spout their ideas of dissension.

Last year there were more than 15,000 of such cases just in Texas alone. The figure today has been reduced to 10,000. Even that number is being depleted, because the NYA is a sort of clearing house for young people wanting jobs.

"We received an order from Fort Worth the other day wanting 60 young boys for office work. We went through our lists and had the boys on the job in a few hours."

State colleges get their apportionment of money. "We don't tell the colleges to whom this money should go. We feel the school officials there know the needs better than we. These officials pick

It used to be, before American civilization became so complex, that a man could bundle up his family in a covered wagon, strike out, and hew out his own destiny in some new country. There were numerous things for the young man coming up to do.

When the depression hit, the plights of American youth, the great throngs that haunted the drug store corners, the pool halls, for lack of something better to do, was brought to the government's attention.

After all, the boy of today was the citizen of tomorrow. If he grew up without an opportunity, the ability that he had would become warped. He would become disgruntled and a unit to be added

the cream of the crop, see that those deserving students get a chance."

The messenger boy comes in and Mr. Johnson takes his feet off the desk. The boy hands him a sheaf of telegrams. They are telegrams from schools, stressing new needs. The drouth is hard here, or the cotton crop has been poor there. All funds will be needed. Please don't forget this or that school.

Mr. Johnson is back at work.

Somewhere, somewhere along the line, another boy will be salvaged from the local gang or the local drug store corner loafer's brigade. He'll be placed in a school room and given a chance to become an active, alert, loyal citizen of a country big enough to look after its youth.

In Mexico on his honeymoon.

Mr. Thomas Jefferson Taylor

announces the marriage of his daughter

Claudia Bird

to

Mr. Lyndon Johnson

on Saturday, the seventeenth of November

One thousand nine hundred and thirty-four

San Antonio, Texas

When Grandpa Fought the Indians

This is another of a series of stories and descriptions which have been prepared—over a period of years—by the convention and publicity bureau of the Chamber of Commerce. One of these stories will be printed each week in the Sunday American-Staesman to inform Central Texas people on what they have in points of interest for tourists in 15 Central Texas counties.

Information in this series has been collected from what is believed to be reliable sources. Any reader differing on details, or having more information, is invited to communicate with the Austin Chamber of Commerce.

As you approach Johnson City a highway 20, after circling rough the vari-hued hills west of ustin, you observe two mountains, at seem by their very formation spell interest. The name of one Lone Man mountain; the other, g mountain.

From the top of Big mountain, miles southeast of Johnson ty, a commanding view may be d of the valley where the famous er creek fight took place in Au-st, 1873.

In those days the settlers were nstntly harassed by marauding dias, who by force or stealth le horses and livestock, or devyed property and took lives.

In this fight, only a relatively w participated on each side. Aft an advance by the Indians, the ites retaliated in a lively skir-sh. Two whites were being taken a ranch (the Johnson home) for ention, one of the boys sum-ned more men to resume the nt, but found that the Indians departed as soon as the whites sed firing.

Many arrow heads have been ked up on this battleground and collection of Dr. C. L. Baskett Johnson City is extensive and uable.

ne-fourth mile off highway 20, Johnson City, is the historic nson home, for which Johnson y is named. It was built in the s, and occupied by Jim, Sam Tom Johnson. The men who re wounded at the Deer creek nt were cared for there. The ians kept Mrs. Sam Johnson d her small daughter under the use for a day and night, and then ve off all the horses that were the ranch, in May, 1873. Adja-t to the log house are several zed rock barns with portholes ough which rifles were probably jected for use against the In-ne.

Where Jim, Sam and Tom Johnson lived back in 18__, when Indians roamed Blanco county. For them the town of Johnson City was named. The old house still stands a quarter mile away from Highway 20 in Johnson City.

Eliza Bunton Johnson as a young matron.

Sam Ealy Johnson Sr
and his elder sister
Frankie Barnett.

In Hays County.

Their first home at Stonewall. Later they built another home about one fourth of a mile from this house. The house above is the one in which Sam Ealy and Rebekah Johnson lived during the first six years of their marriage and is the birthplace of Lyndon.

About 1914

Have You Met

Sam Johnson State Inspector

THE RAILROAD COMMISSION is to be congratulated on the appointment of Sam Johnson of Blanco County as Inspector for the Motor Transportation Division. The long and efficient public career of Mr. Johnson especially fits him for work of this character.

Beginning as a school teacher at an early age, he taught school for two years before entering a law office for study. He was elected to the legislature in 1904, being one of the youngest members of that body, and served twelve years as member of the lower house. During his tenure of office, Mr. Johnson was the author of much constructive legislation and was often complimented on his ability as a lawmaker by such men as A. W. Terrell, John M. Duncan, Jim Robinson, Thomas B. Love and many other leading members of the House with which he served

He is the author of the Alamo Purchase Bill and of the bill providing for the erection of a home for the widows of Confederate soldiers, hav-

ing been selected by the Daughters of the Republic and the Daughters of the Confederacy to sponsor these bills. In 1917 he was the author of a bill appropriating $3,000,000 to help the drouth-stricken people of West Texas. The Johnson Blue Sky Law of Texas affords an example of his constructive statesmanship.

During the 38th Legislature he was appointed by the speaker of the house to serve as chairman of the committee on municipal and private corporations. Since his appointment as motor bus inspector, he has heard and adjusted many difficulties arising from the enforcement of these laws. His diplomacy, his knowledge of conditions throughout the State, his tact in dealing with men, his sound judgment, untiring energy and agreeable personality render him especially qualified for this position.

Rebekah Baines
Johnson.

At four in Austin.

In schooldays.

In 1917

Christmas - 1936.

Sam and his sons.

Off to Congress.

'Home' to Lyndon Johnson

When the Johnson family left their farm and moved in to their ancestral home of Johnson City it was to this house that they moved. Lyndon was a boy of five then. It has been his home ever since and it is to it he returns between sessions of congress.

Johnson's Election as U. S. Senator to

Playing and Working Hard Characteristics of Texan

Candidate Product of Political Background With Two Forebears Members of Legislature

BY T. A. PRICE.

Grandpaw Sam Johnson knew it more than thirty-two years ago.

On Oct. 27, 1908, the Texas pioneer who founded Johnson City in Blanco County, was called to the home of his son to see his new grandson and, after viewing the babe resting on his mother's breast, he said:

"He's a fine child. He'll be a United States Senator some day."

That was Lyndon Baines Johnson's welcome to the little farm home near Stonewall, in Gillespie County, where Sam Johnson Jr. had taken his bride, Rebecca Baines Johnson, following their marriage at Blanco.

Under the watchful eye of a mother whose sense of parental responsibility was great, and under the careful guidance of a father proud of the fact that in his son's veins flowed the blood of two great Texas families, Lyndon grew as fast as the jackrabbits of the hills he roamed in his boyhood.

Goes to College.

The family moved to Johnson City in 1913, when Lyndon was 5 years old, and there he grew to manhood. Blanco County elementary schools prepared him for the Johnson City High School, whence he was graduated in 1926.

Here followed two years of adolescent indecision. Study had palled. There was a trip to California with some other boys. There was a period of working on the county highways. Then, with ambition reawakened after a heart-to-heart talk with his father, the youth set out for San Marcos and the state teacher college there to wrangle a B. S. degree in a little more than two years while he worked as janitor and college secretary and on the highways during his vacations to pay his way.

Background for all of Lyndon Johnson's youthful activities, however, had been politics. Both his father and his grandfather were leaders in the community and both represented the district in the Legislature.

Works, Plays Hard.

From very infancy a dynamo of physical as well as mental force, the boy missed nothing that happened in his environment. He loved to work. When he played he played hard. Always he was a leader of the crowd with whom he grew.

Sailing far above the clouds in an airplane between San Antonio and Houston, the new United States Senator from Texas reminisced with the writer of those boyhood days which still are very near to him. Always his mother or his father was the center of every picture that he drew.

The elder Johnson was a keen trader but open-handed and open-hearted in his generosity.

"One time he bought a paper," the youthful statesman chuckled as he leaned across the aisle of the plane. "He didn't need a paper and didn't want one. But the editor was ill and had been told by his doctor to go to Arizona. So papa bought the business.

"Then he turned it over to mamma to run. At that time I had gone in business, too. I had set up a shoe-shine stand in the barbershop and was out for big money when a speaker came to town and delivered a lecture in which the theme was it pays to advertise. I drank in the words of this stranger and then, went to my mother and bought space on the front page of her paper to advertise my bootblack stand.

"Papa had been on a trip and returned just in time to catch one of the first papers off the press. He was so astounded that he for years told the story of buying a paper so that his wife could advertise the fact that his son was a bootblack."

Impatient With Studies.

Impatience with his studies in school was a characteristic of this active boy, but his mother would give him no rest. For every artifice he set up to dodge his studies she found another that was effective in making him learn. Tales of this period are told by both the new Senator and his mother and one may read between the lines how determination was met by determination, with the strong will of the pioneer woman finally victorious.

"Many times," Mrs. Johnson confided with a smile, "I would not catch up with the fact that Lyndon was not prepared on a lesson until breakfast time of a school day. Then I would get the book and place it on the table before his father and devote the whole breakfast period to a discussion of what my son should have learned the night before, not with Lyndon but with my husband.

"Of course Lyndon was too well trained to interrupt this table talk, and, forced to listen, he would learn. That way, and by following him to the gate nearly every morning and telling him tales of history and geography and algebra, I could see that he was prepared for the work of the day."

Expedition to California.

Graduation from high school Lyndon Johnson took as a happy release from years of drudgery. He had no thought of college, and to forestall any chance of being forced to attend an institution of higher learning he organized a band of his fellows into an expedition to California.

"That was a great trip," the lanky statesman grinned boyishly. "None of us had been off the farm for a trip longer than the road to town. I started with $18 and few of the party had more. We'd camp out along the railroad tracks at night and always our first chore would be to dig a hole in which to bury our money.

"This interment of the funds was an every evening ritual and always the heaviest member of the party was assigned to sleep over the cache. We didn't propose to be robbed.

"But in spite of all this care we came to a place where a hole no longer was necessary. The money we had—a sum in the aggregate which had seemed huge at the start —just trickled away. When we were broke and job hunting caused us to separate.

Goes on Diet.

"That was the time I went on a diet," Johnson chuckled over a cup of tomato juice which had just been handed him by a pretty air hostess. "Nothing to eat was the principal item on my food chart. Up and down the coast I tramped, washing dishes, waiting on table, doing farm work when it was available and always growing thinner.

"The trip back home was the longest I have ever made. Maybe that's why I like to fly now. I certainly prayed for wings during those long days."

Back home the idea of study still was repugnant, so young Lyndon got him a job with a road gang, where he shoveled material and drove a truck and pushed a wheelbarrow and grew calouses on his hands until one day his father talked to him about it.

"It's fine to be satisfied with the simple things," Sam Johnson told his son gently. "A man who is satisfied to be a laborer will never have much on his mind. Of course there won't be much in it, but those who are willing to devote all their lives to a road job really don't need much."

It was a canny hint. Lyndon went and told his mother about it and she smiled. The next day he wrapped up his clothes and started for San Marcos.

He had borrowed a little money on his own note. He got a job as janitor that was just as hard on the hands as his road work. And he didn't like it so he set out to make the strain as short as possible. Those were the days when the man who was destined to succeed to the toga of Morris Sheppard learned that he was capable of prodigies of concentration on study.

He learned to sweep the halls of San Marcos State Teachers College in less time than it ever had been done before, other chores were timed to the same accellerated pace. That saved him the hours required to act as college secretary and for study and more study.

Recited Lessons Aloud.

With the family tradition of politics always in his mind, the young man who had scorned higher education now became a human sponge for the absorption of knoledge. Facts were his meat and bread. He recited his lessons aloud as he worked alone after other students had left the school. He practiced oratory in the halls which he kept clean. He made speeches to walls as he wiped them down. He told tales of the ancients to the door mats which he shook free from dust.

And it was here in San Marcos, as he strove to qualify for a new opinion from his father, under the influence of a mother who had encouraged him to do it, that he met the other woman who was to be a great influence in his life; the woman who has to take up and carry on the spurring of ambition which had been until now his mother's job. That woman was Miss Claudia Taylor, daughter of T. J. Taylor of Karnak. Of course no one knew her as Claudia. She had been rechristened Lady Bird by her old Negro nurse and she had become Lady Bird at school. Since then she has been Lady Bird in Austin and Washington and Saturday's election made her Lady Bird to a nation that was watching the progress of this Texas election.

After his graduation from San Marcos in 1930 Lyndon Johnson joined the faculty of the Sam

Houston High School in Houston, where he taught public speaking and debating for two years and where many of the young men and young women who had been members of his classes turned out Friday night to swell the great crowd in the Coliseum there which gave him an ovation such as has seldom been seen in a political race in this state.

When Richard M. Kleberg was elected to Congress in 1933 he took Lyndon Johnson to Washington with him as his secretary, and it was while on that job that the native state to take as his wife the girlhood sweetheart who had been earning two college degrees while waiting for him.

Made Many Friends.

In Washington young Johnson made many friends. He was personable. In all the 6 feet 3 inches of his typically Texan physique he personified an old-fashioned courtesy and kindness.

By 1935 he had won the attention of President Franklin D. Roosevelt and he was appointed as state administrator for the National Youth Administration. Here, leading young Johnson won his first national fame. The organization he built in Texas became a model on which other units were based in states all over the nation.

"Those were great days," he told me, as his eyes lit up with the pleasure of the reminiscence. "Those kids came into the units as we established them, railing at fortune and circumstance and cowed by the economic conditions that had left them without a job and without the means to live on the self-supporting, independent basis that should be every American boy's and

girl's birthright. And their frowns soon were changed to smiles.

"For a time after we began the work I tried to be the first person on the job every morning, but I found that by trying to do so I had just set up a contest. They were as anxious to get there as I was. They were as anxious to show that all they had lacked was opportunity as I was anxious to have them show it.

"Skills grew with practice and opportunities came to them as they perfected these skills. If the Roosevelt administration had done never another thing it would have been justified by the work of this great institution for the salvation of youth.

"When our district's well-loved Representative in Congress, James P. Buchanan, died, I heeded the advice of my friends—the same home folks who always had stood behind me—and ran for the office as one of a field of eleven and was elected.

Re-elected Without Opposition.

"Since that time I have been re-elected twice without opposition. I feel that the principal qualification which I had shown for the office was my work for the NYA."

Lyndon Johnson's career in Congress was meteoric. While still in the ranks in Texas outside his own district he was widely known over the nation by those who keep a close eye on national legislative affairs. He became a member of the powerful House naval affairs committee and soon made himself such a force on that body that it was not hard for him to influence the establishment of the great $45,000,-000 naval air training base at Corpus Christi, which is destined to be the largest in the nation.

Here Lyndon was born in the west bedroom
with the fireplace and windows shaded by a tree.

Uncle Berry Roebuck who drove cattle to Kansas with Lyndon's grandfather, Sam Johnson, shows Lynda Bird where her great grandmother, Eliza Bunton Johnson, hid under the house during an Indian raid.

Lyndon looks very much like his father in this picture

Lyndon, Bird, Lynda Bird, Mr. Roebuck, Uncle Tom and Lyndon's mother visit the old landmark.

Lyndon Baines Johnson's
Grandparents

Ruth Ament Huffman

Ruth Ament Huffman, fifth of the eight daughters of Dr. John Smith and Mary Elizabeth (Perrin) Huffman, was born near Rowlett, Collin County, Texas, December 10, 1854. She inherited the blond coloring, sunny disposition, and genial friendliness of her father, and the fortitude and domestic abilities of her mother.

She loved to romp with her sisters, her only brother, and her gay and handsome father, to ride at full speed across the farm on one of her father's fine Kentucky horses, to go on Sunday in stiffly starched petticoats and freshly curled ringlets in the big hack to church and Sunday School, and to learn the housewifely arts under the efficient tutelage of her mother.

She attended school at the one-room school and church at Rowlett. She was a demure and obedient pupil, conscientious but only mildly interested, save for her love of geography and poetry. The loss of her adored father at the close of the Civil War, following arduous service as a Confederate surgeon and deep anxiety for his family, brought great sorrow to Ruth, as well as great changes in the family circumstances.

In 1869, just before the opening of school, Ruth's mother was greatly surprised to receive a call from the young school teacher, Joseph W. Baines, who had been teaching at Rowlett two years. He asked for her permission "to pay his addresses" to her daughter, Ruth. The comely widow with a house full of marriageable daughters, while astounded by his choice of one so young, was greatly pleased. Ruth, herself, most surprised of all, as she had thought "Teacher" rather severe with her, was not, on reflection, averse to the idea. Shortly before her fifteenth birthday, on Sunday morning, September 12, 1869, at Rowlett church, the young Joseph Baines and Ruth Huffman were married. It was a beautiful wedding, the lovely young bride and her six bridesmaids were lovely. After the ceremony performed by Rev. Long, all repaired to the home of the bride's grandfather, "Grand-daddy" John S. Huffman, for a sumptuous dinner. This was the beginning of the happiest of marriages to continue for nearly forty years. The young couple boarded at Captain Bush's home for a while, and then at "Grand-daddy's". Then they acquired a little home at Plano and took into their household, the bride's young sister, Rebekah, for company for Ruth and to assist in relieving the straitened circumstances in her mother's home.

Ruth grew in beauty and acquired housewifely skill. She was five feet two inches in height, with a wealth of golden curls, fair skin, and grey eyes. She was amiable, gentle and affectionate. In 1870, Joseph Baines moved to McKinney to study and practice law, and to edit a newspaper. There, in June 1881, nearly twelve years after their marriage, their first child, Rebekah, was born. In 1883, they moved to Austin to live for four years where, in April 1884, their second child, a son, Huffman was born. In January 1887, the little family moved to Blanco, where Joseph W. Baines practiced law until 1904 in that and adjoining counties. This was a happy period for the family, now increased, in 1889, by a little daughter, Josefa, named for her father. Always active in the Baptist church with which she had united at an early age, Ruth was a beloved Sunday School teacher. She was never seen with idle hands, was an excellent seamstress, the best of cooks, a spotless housekeeper, and a wonderful homemaker.

After the family's removal to Fredericksburg in 1904, following financial strain and increased impairment of her hearing, though circumstances were less happy, Ruth retained her cheerfulness and energy. A great blow came in the increasing illness and death of her beloved husband on November 18, 1906. The fortitude and resourcefulness she showed in these dark hours amazed all who knew her. She sold the little home which her husband had built in his last months of life and moved with her youngest child to San Marcos, Texas, where she boarded college students for several years. Later on, she made her home with her son, making extended visits to her daughters and other relatives. She died at his home in San Antonio, Texas, February 13, 1936 and was buried by the side of her husband in Fredericksburg cemetery.

She had a keen zest for living, boundless energy, a cheerful optimism, and great interest in all about her. Sensible, practical-minded, thrifty, yet generous, she gave freely of her means and services. She loved to quote: "Wilful waste makes woeful want"; "The Lord helps them who help themselves"; "Whatsoever thy hand findeth to do, do it with all they might". Her daily life was an exemplification of these sayings. Literal minded, she could never understand a joke, though she loved laughter and fun. She was one of the neatest and most carefully groomed of women. Her beautiful hair, with its waves, golden in youth, brown in maturity, and snow-white in old age, was always carefully arranged, and a fresh dress with a gold bar pin at her throat was donned before she put on a clean apron and began cooking breakfast for her family. She had a long, rich life, full of love and work and happiness. She spoke ill of no one, was incapable of guile, and her heart was pure and trusting.

Samuel Ealy Johnson Sr.

Somewhere in Alabama, the tenth child of Jesse Johnson and his wife, Lucy Webb Barnett, Samuel Ealy Johnson was born, November 12th, 1838. His parents were residents of Georgia during the greater part of their lives, living in Greene, Henry and Oglethorpe Counties. In 1846, Jesse Johnson brought his family to Texas, settling in Lockhart, Texas where he died in 1856, his wife surviving him by only a year.

Young Sam, orphaned at 18, with his brother, Tom (Jesse Thomas), for whom he held great admiration and close attachment until Tom's death in 1877, became deeply interested and actively engaged in the cattle business. In 1859 the brothers were buying cattle and pasturing them at Fredericksburg, Texas, before driving them on to Kansas. They were mentioned in "Trail Drivers of Texas" as being the largest individual trail drivers operating in 1870 in Blanco, Gillespie, Llano, Burnet, Hays, Comal and Kendall Counties, with headquarter pens and branding stall at the mouth of Williamson's Creek in Blanco County, and headquarters at Johnson's Ranch on the Pedernales River at Johnson City, the county seat site of Blanco County. They drove cattle to Kansas and Montana in 1870, 1871, 1872, and 1873.

In the late '50's, the Johnson brothers established headquarters at Johnson City, where they built a log cabin with portholed rock barn, the first settlement of that section, later to become a landmark of Texas.

On September 18, 1861, Sam Ealy Johnson enlisted at Lockhart, Texas in Company B, De Bray's Regiment, C.S.A., and served through the Civil War. He was at the Battle of Galveston and had his horse killed under him at Pleasant Hill in 1862. He was a man of high physical courage and strong nerve and carried a wounded companion on his back from the battlefield, with great danger to himself; held wounded soldiers during amputations; and did many other acts of bravery requiring strong physical control and love for his fellow-soldiers.

Returning to Lockhart and Johnson City after the War, he resumed cattle buying and trail driving to Abilene, Kansas and other market points. In Lockhart, December 11, 1867, he married Miss Eliza Bunton, daughter of Lieutenant Robert Desha Bunton and his wife, Jane McIntosh. The young couple set up housekeeping in the log cabin at Johnson City, where Sam and Tom had "bached" before the War, the headquarters for their cattle drives. Indians were active in this section during this period. On August 15, 1869, Mr. and Mrs. Tom Felps, near Cypress Creek, Blanco County, were killed and scalped by Indians. The countryside was aroused and a few days later ten young men of this section met a band of Indians, and engaged in the battle of Deer Creek, in which the Indians were routed. Alexander and George Roberts and Joe Bird were wounded and carried to the Johnson Ranch for attention.

Shortly after this, Sam and Eliza Johnson moved to Caldwell County and later to Hays County, where they resided until about 1889, when they returned to the "mountains", settling on the Pedernales River about twelve miles from Johnson City. All but the eldest of their nine children were born at Buda, Hays County, and attended school there Several became teachers and taught in Blanco and nearby counties.

Sam Johnson was reared a Baptist, joined the Christian Church in early manhood, but in his later years affiliated with the Christadelphians. He was a consistent and devout member of this church until his death from pneumonia, at Stonewall, Texas on February 25th, 1915.

Highly gregarious, he attended all the neighborly gatherings and met his friends with a handshake, friendly greetings and a hearty resounding laugh. He seldom returned from these gatherings without accompanying guests, and was widely known for his hospitality and kind friendliness. A man of strong courage, deep convictions and a calm philosophy which allowed no worry, he lived serenely and quietly at his pleasant country home on the bank of the Pedernales, from 1888 to 1915, almost thirty years. Prior to that, he led a very active, energetic, often hazardous, existence. He was a tall, lithe, well-built, rangy man, six feet in height, with black wavy hair and blue eyes. His snowy beard and thick mane of white hair in his last years gave him a patriarchal appearance.

He loved to sit on the front porch of his farm home reading his Bible and the newspapers, and greeting the frequent visitors with a hearty invitation to get down and come right in for a good visit. Although he had a high temper, he was seldom seen in anger and never in his life used an oath. He had a very deep and abiding faith in the Christadelphian creed, and, when dying, fully conscious, spoke to his loved ones, assuring them of his complete readiness to meet his Maker and of his sustaining hope of eternal life. His death, as his life, was an inspiration to those who knew him.

—Bibliography: The Trail Drivers of Texas, P. 329
History of Blanco County, J. W. Speer, Chap. 15, P. 53

THE JOHNSON FAMILY
by T. U. Taylor

There was a Johnson family who lived near the present town of Johnson City, and whose frontier home is still standing; Tom Johnson and his younger brother, Samuel Ealy Johnson, born in Georgia in 1838, settled in the Pedernales Valley and bought land in Blanco County before the Civil War. Here they built a log cabin and lived for several years, while driving cattle to Kansas, Montana, and Wyoming. It was the first settlement at the site of Johnson City, and was known as Johnson's Ranch. Tom and Sam Johnson had associated with them three nephews, Jesse, John and James Johnson. The five Johnsons had a rather loose partnership, one of the articles of which was to the effect that if one member of the firm should marry, he should check out of the firm, take his share, and then go it alone. One of the nephews, James Johnson, drew the plot of land east of the creek in Johnson City, and when the town was laid off, it was on James Johnson's land; and thus we have Johnson City. Mrs. O. Y. Fawcett, a daughter of James Johnson, is living in Johnson City today and carrying on the traditions of the Johnson family.

The house is still standing, with its rock barn portholes for defense against the Indians, and is one of the historical landmarks of Texas. To this log house, in 1867, Samuel Ealy Johnson brought his bride, Eliza Bunton.

Eliza Bunton Johnson

Eliza Bunton, the fourth child of Robert Holmes and Priscilla Jane McIntosh Bunton, was born at Russellville, Logan County, Kentucky, June 24, 1849. About ten years later she came with her parents to

Lockhart, Caldwell County, Texas, where she resided until her marriage there, December 11, 1867, to Sam Ealy Johnson.

Her honeymoon and earliest years of married life were spent at her husband's ranch, where Johnson City now stands. Later, after a brief residence in Caldwell County, she and her husband moved to Buda, Hays County, Texas, where they resided until 1889, when they returned to the hill country, settling near Stonewall, Gillespie County, Texas, on a farm on the Pedernales River. In 1870, the Sam Johnsons and their baby daughter, Mary, moved to Buda, where their nine children were reared and attended school. These were prosperous days, but very busy ones. With six little girls to keep in starched pinafores and three boys in seemly attire, with all her household and social duties, Eliza had little time for rest. She was glad to move to the mountains where the tempo of life was slower. The children, too, were growing older. Mary, the eldest, had married Ed Walling and remained on the prairie. The others began to leave the home, to teach, to marry, to make lives of their own.

One February morning in 1912, Eliza sat sewing a button on her husband's shirt; she gave a cry and fell from her chair. She had suffered a stroke, from which she never fully recovered. Death came to her at the farm home, January 30, 1917. She was laid to rest by her husband's side in the family graveyard near the home.

Eliza Bunton was tall with patrician bearing, high-bred features, raven hair, piercing black eyes, and magnolia-white skin. Reserved and modest, she hated flattery and insincerity and had no personal vanity. Of a serious, thoughtful nature, and a selflessness of purpose, she spent her life span of nearly sixty-eight years in devoted service to her family. "Charity begins at home", she often quoted, and was ever quick to respond to the need of any of her children. From the depths of the big zinc trunk, which held her treasures and her meeting clothes, she would bring out an old purse, holding the egg-and-butter money carefully saved for the purchase of a new black silk dress, and count out the exact amount needed by the child temporarily financially embarrassed. Sometimes the purse was left empty, but she eagerly assured the recipient of the loan of her happiness to be of service and her own lack of present need. She had no pride of earthly possessions, and all references to the handsome clothes and the elegant furniture of more prosperous days were casual, never complaining nor regretful. It was said that when reverses came, she sold her silver-mounted carriage and matched span of horses, a gift from "Brother Tom", her husband's favorite brother, and made a payment on the place in the hill country that was to become the family home.

She honored the good and the great and was proud of the part her people had had in the upbuilding of our nation. With quiet dignity and modest pride, she admonished her children to be worthy of their glorious heritage of courageous and unselfish patriotism, as exemplified in the life of her illustrious uncle, John W. Bunton, and many others of their ancestry. She loved her household duties; no one else could bake home-made bread with such appetizing aroma and tastiness, or churn quite such golden butter. She read her Bible every day and followed its teachings as she interpreted them. Her heart belonged to her God and her family.

HEROINES OF THE HIGHLANDS OF SOUTHWEST TEXAS
Leading Women Among the Pioneers, Chapter IV, by T. U. Taylor

Among the many leading pioneer women of Blanco County are included the following: Mrs. Joseph Bird, Mrs. Tom Felps, Mrs. Samuel Johnson (Eliza Bunton).

Eliza Bunton, a daughter of Robert Desha Bunton, a niece of John Wheeler Bunton, signer of the Declaration of Independence and Constitution of Texas, and a member of the first congress and a hero of San Jacinto. Eliza Bunton was gently reared but she took to the frontier life like the heroine she was, and became a member of that hall of fame that should be erected to the heroines of the highlands of Southwest Texas. She often saw horses dash into the pens near the house with arrows sticking in their flanks. She saw horses and cattle stolen from these pens and, to this day of the year of 1940, a visitor can see the place where she crept under the floor to hide during the raids of the Red Warriors. During the memorable Deer Creek fight about three miles from Johnson City, two men were wounded and taken to the home of Samuel Ealy Johnson and were cared for and nursed by his heroine wife, Eliza Bunton Johnson.

Like all pioneer women, she baked her bread on the old baker, or rather, Texas skillet that had a top to it, and on the old fire place. She had her old ash hopper, saved her lye and grease and in the spring had soft soap that soon became hard under the skilled manipulation of frontier women.

Mrs. Eliza Bunton Johnson was a beautiful young woman with piercing black eyes, coal black hair, queenly in her carriage, a woman of great refinement and strong family pride. She loved to talk of her cousins, Governor Joseph Desha of Kentucky, John W. Breckenridge, Miss Mary Desha, co-founder of the Daughters of the American Revolution, and her brother Joe Bunton who, with his lifelong friend, Governor Joseph B. Sayers, fought with the immortal Texas Rangers, of which George W. Littlefield was an honored member. Samuel Ealy Johnson was a member of De Bray's Regiment and fought throughout the Civil War. Samuel Ealy Johnson and his wife, Eliza Bunton Johnson had nine children.

Joseph Wilson Baines
by George W. Baines

Joseph Wilson Baines, third son of the Elder Rev. G. W. Baines, and his wife, Melissa Ann, was born in Mt. Lebanon, La., January 24, 1846. From 1850 he spent his life in Texas. Anderson Academy and Baylor

University (at Independence), furnished his educational opportunities, which, however, were cut short by the Civil War, in which he was engaged the last two years. When the war closed he traveled horseback over nearly all the settled sections of the State, endeavoring to make collections on accounts due his father as editor and publisher of the old Texas Baptist, the first paper the Baptists of this State had. But little money was realized, and the notes given, amounting to several thousand dollars, were all cancelled in a year or two, by father. I have now in my possession, stacks of these notes, in the beautiful writing of my brother, and cancelled by father, because he would lay no further burden on his brethren, impoverished by the war.

In 1867 Brother Joe began teaching school on Rowlett's Creek, in Collin County. He and Miss Ruth, daughter of Dr. John and Mary Huffman, were married in 1869. Inclined to the law, he studied under the famous firm of Throckmorton and Brown, of McKinney, for whom he formed an ardent and life-long attachment. Beginning his practice in Plano, later he moved to McKinney, where he successfully engaged in his profession, and also published and edited the Advocate, a widely read and influential Democratic paper.

During the four years' governorship of Hon. John Ireland, my brother was Secretary of State, discharging the duties of that office with perfect satisfaction to all concerned, and making many friends by his cheerfulness and efficiency. Gov. Ireland had so much confidence in his character and ability that he gave over to him the writing of his life, an undertaking that he cheerfully accepted, as he also did the life of Gov. Throckmorton. The lives of these distinguished Texans have not yet been published; and I do not know that they were ever made entirely ready for the press.

In 1887, my brother, ever fond of a quiet and simple life, settled in Blanco, then the county seat of Blanco County, where he had an extensive and lucrative civil practice, accumulating, in course of time, quite a fortune. He became a member of the 27th Legislature, where he soon came to be regarded as one of the most faithful and capable members of that body.

On account of disastrous drouths, protracted four years, his extensive farming operations brought financial ruin. Believing that Fredericksburg, a thriving German town, offered fine opportunities for successful practice, he moved there some two years ago. He quickly won the confidence of the sturdy Germans, and when taken sick, had all the business that he could well handle. By too close attention to office work, a malignant liver trouble was induced, which after about three months, resulted in his death, Sunday morning, 8:20, November 18th. His wife, his son and two daughters and myself were with him and saw him fall asleep. His funeral occurred in the German Methodist Church, and was conducted by Brother Cohron, the Baptist pastor at Kerrville, who braved a keenly cold norther for thirty miles in order to honor our dead, and comfort our aching hearts. We shall never cease to love him for his brotherly service.

Thus is given in brief outline a life of more than 60 years.

If Brother Cranfill had not asked for this sketch for The Tribune, I could not have undertaken it, for two reasons: First, the task is too painful, and then I sorely distrust myself to write justly of my brother. Perhaps few brothers were ever so intimate and devoted as we. From childhood, more than two years my senior, he ever seemed to me near perfection's mark; and all through life exercised a happy and forceful influence upon his younger brother. As the family circle narrowed, through the passing years, until he and I alone remained in Texas, we became more and more devotedly attached. For many years it had been our happy dream that, when old age should enforce retirement from active life, we might spend our last years near each other. But "God's finger touched him and he slept."

Joseph Wilson Baines was the highest type of citizen; public-spirited, profoundly concerned for the welfare of the people, strong in love for justice and righteousness, above all sham and meanness, high in ideals and absolutely clean in life. He had the noble faculty of winning and holding confidence. He was gentle and brave, generous and brotherly. During his sickness and after his death, it was simply beautiful to see how deeply his German neighbors, on every side, were affected. In most appropriate ways did they give tokens of their tender appreciation of the man, who, in so short a time, had won their hearts.

Patient, persistent and happy hopefulness were prominent characteristics. Courageously and without murmur he bore his own burdens, never inflicting them upon others, while he also sympathetically bore the burdens of others, thus fulfilling the law of Christ. As near as any man that I ever knew did he come to obeying Paul's injunction, to be "diligent in business, fervent in spirit, serving the Lord". To him honor meant much. To be right was ever more than to win. His law partner for many years, Mr. Nat Stubbs, said to me: "In our consultations about cases, he was always more concerned about doing right and acting honorable than he was about the success of the suit".

As a lawyer, he was not brilliant, but he was thorough. He was not overwhelming in argument, but he was clear, strong and convincing. With indefatigable industry and patient investigation, he mastered his cases. His evident sincerity, magnanimous conduct and fair dealing, won him friends, even if he lost his case.

My brother's home life was singularly beautiful and happy. His marriage was most felicitous in every respect. His devotion to his wife and children, and their devotion to him made a spectacle for angels. Home to him was the happiest place in the whole world. The well-being and pleasure of his family were his greatest earthly concerns. After he lost his fortune, by over-kindness to farm tenants and by overconfidence in men he resolutely set about re-making a bountiful and beautiful home for his dear ones. In doing this he overtaxed his constitution and fell a victim to his devotion. It may well be doubted, that if in all the land there was a more loving, trustful and happy family than his. Above all, his was a Christian home, in which piety was practiced, the old doctrines of the Bible believed and taught, God loved and honored. His wife and children walked with him in the way of the Lord.

My brother's Christian life was steady and strong. Modesty kept him in the background until conscious duty brought him forward; then he stood exactly where he was needed. Ever liberal with his means, ever true to his pastor and church, ever prompt in all his religious engagements, there was little that could be added to his Christian character. He was a Baptist, strict in doctrine, broad in charity, large in enterprise. For well nigh twenty years, he was the chief pillar in the Blanco Church, and after he brought his family to Fredericksburg he obtained letters, intending, with his family, to join a church some 12 miles in the country, it being the nearest Baptist church to him. With great joy he confidently looked forward to the time when there would be a church of his own faith with a good meetinghouse in Fredericksburg, and he had even selected the lot on which the house should be built. He had one characteristic as a Christian that I emphasize with great pleasure, and that was his cleanness. He hated dirt, he loved neatness. For clean speech and morals, he could hardly have been surpassed. To hear a preacher indulge in unclean jokes or suggestions gave him a real disgust, and he never wanted to hear him preach or pray. Converted and baptized when ten years of age, he grew up a model man in all noble qualities. I could not wish to have a more tender and affectionate brother. So long as he lived, I knew that there was at least one person who would not let me or mine suffer, if his ability could prevent.

When I helped to dress him for the grave, I thought of how, at ten years of age, he was baptized in a shroud, made some weeks before when it was expected that he would surely die, and of how he is now clothed in white and holds a palm in his hand.

Alpine, Texas.   —The Baptist Tribune, December 13, 1906.

THE HANDBOOK OF TEXAS
The Texas State Historical Association, P. 96.

Joseph Wilson Baines, son of George W. Baines, was born in Bienville Parish, Louisiana in the middle 1840's. He moved with his parents to Independence, Texas, where he was educated. During the Civil War he served with W. M. Williamson's cadets. In 1867 Joseph Baines moved to Collin County, where he taught school for three years, and where he married Ruth A. Huffman at McKinney on September 12, 1869. Admitted to the bar, he practiced law at Plano in 1870, and later at McKinney. In 1877 he established McKinney Advocate. From January 1873 until 1877 he was Secretary of State under Governor John Ireland. Baines practiced law at Blanco from 1888 to 1903, when he moved to Fredericksburg. He was survived by his wife and three children when he died at Fredericksburg, on November 18, 1906.

—Bibliography: W. N. Ramey, Texian Annual (1886);
McKinney Weekly Democrat, Nov. 22, 1906, and Aug. 14, 1930.

Brown eyed, with soft brown waving hair, and a complexion tending to ruddiness, the young Joe, or Josie, Baines was a slender, personable young man about five feet ten in height. His lofty brown and serious expression belied the keen sense of humor which animated his conversation. He loved beauty, particularly in the fields of nature and literature. A basket of fruit gathered from his orchard came to the breakfast table under his deft hands, a study in color and arrangement. His sense of organization was excellent. Everything had its place, not only in the office and his home, but in everything he touched. "Find the best way to do a thing and always do it that way", he said.

As a teacher, he was incomparable, always first determining the principle behind the problem, and presenting it so clearly and forcibly that understanding was unquestionable. He had a great facility of expression, selecting always the word which expressed most exactly his meaning.

He had a deep interest in government and politics and read widely along those lines, and always proudly said, "I am a Baptist and a Democrat".

Eliza Bunton Johnson and
her mother, Priscilla Jane
Bunton.

Sam Easly Johnson Jr his parents and his brother George, far right.

Starting to "meeting" Sunday morning.

Joseph Wilson Baines   *Ruth Ament (Huffman) Baines.*

Amenthal, Their home at Blanco, Texas.

Joseph Wilson Baines.

Lyndon Baines Johnson's
Great Grandparents

Jesse Johnson

Jesse Johnson, the third son of John Johnson, was born in Oglethorpe County, Georgia, April 28, 1795. On November 14, 1817 he married Lucy Webb Barnett, daughter of Leonard Barnett in Greene County, Georgia. In 1824, and again in 1828, he served as sheriff of Henry County. He was engaged in farming in Oglethorpe, Henry and Greene Counties in Georgia, save for a brief residence in 1838 in Alabama. In 1846, he and his wife came to Texas. His second son, Nathan Barnett Johnson, born in 1820, a physician, and his eldest daughter, Ava Ann (Johnson) Adams, born in 1822, remained in Henry County, Georgia.

The Johnsons located at Lockhart, Caldwell County, Texas and purchased a home there. The eldest son, John Leonard Johnson, a physician, with his wife and children located at Gonzales, Texas. The other three sons, Andrew Jackson Johnson, Thomas Jesse Johnson, and Samuel Ealy Johnson, the youngest, born in 1838, while very young engaged in the cattle business.

The daughters: Amanda, who married a Kelly; Frankie who became Mrs. Leonard Barnett; Betty, who married a Texas hero, Thomas Hunt; and Lucy, the youngest who married a McCarthy, all found widely-separated Texas homes in due time. In 1854, Jesse Johnson's health began to fail, and on May 15, 1856, he passed away at his home in Lockhart, Texas.

He was a man of great charity and kindness and took into his home the five children of his eldest son when their mother died; and for some time reared these children with his own. He was energetic, public spirited, interested in politics and government, devoted to his family, his town, and his church. He was a consistent member of the Baptist church. He was of English descent.

LAST WILL AND TESTAMENT OF JESSE JOHNSON

Filed in my office for probate September 22, A.D. 1856.

> —Saml J. P. McDowell
> Clerk, County Court House, Caldwell County

Filed for record 3 o'clock P.M., December 30, 1856.

> —Saml J. P. McDowell

THE STATE OF TEXAS, GONZALES COUNTY.

Know all men by these presents That I, Jesse Johnson, of the County of Caldwell and State aforesaid, am at this time at J. L. Johnson's (my son) house, and viewing my situation as extremely critical and being in a diseased condition and perhaps may be suddenly taken worse and be deprived from making a will so as to protect my companion and while in my right mind have thought proper to make this my last will. Item 1, I wish J. L. Johnson and A. J. Johnson, my sons, to act as my executors. Item 2, I wish all my legal debts to be paid. Item 3, I wish all my stock of cattle and horses, excepting such as are claimed by the children, to be sold for the purpose of paying the debts. Item 4, I will that all my property is to remain as it is, excepting the stock named in Item 3 during my wife's, Lucy W. Johnson, lifetime and to be subject to her control in her lifetime. Item 5, I will that at her death that all my property be equally divided between my children, excepting the heirs of Nathan B. Johnson of the State of Georgia, who I will to have one thousand dollars more than my other heirs, the balance to be equally divided between the other heirs. Given under my hand this 30 August 1854.

> —*Jesse Johnson*

R. L. McCorkle
J. T. Johnson
(depose as witnesses)

Lucy Webb Barnett

Lucy Webb Barnett, the daughter of Leonard and Nancy (Statham) Barnett was born in Georgia, probably in Elbert County, on January 14, 1798. One brother, Pleasant L. Barnett is mentioned in early records, but it is believed that she had other brothers and some sisters. She moved with her parents to Greene County, Georgia, and there on November 14, 1817 married Jesse Johnson. The young couple resided in Greene, Henry, and Oglethorpe Counties, Georgia for nearly thirty years. In 1846, they came to Texas and located at Lockhart, Texas. There, March 13, 1857, Lucy passed away at the age of fifty-seven. Only one of her ten children had preceded her in death. She was laid to rest by the side of her husband, Jesse, who had died in May of the preceding year.

Robert Holmes Bunton

Robert Holmes Bunton was born September 7, 1818 in Sumner County, Tennessee. He was the seventh child of Joseph Robert and Phoebe (Desha) Bunton. His early life was spent in Tennessee and Kentucky where he removed with his family. In 1840, he married Priscilla Jane McIntosh, daughter of James William and Julia Ann (Miller) McIntosh at Russellville, Kentucky. He was a substantial planter. In Kentucky, seven of his eight children were born: Mollie, who married Matt Copenhover and died about 1878 in Texas; Joseph Lloyd, who served in Terry's Texas Rangers; John Desha, who died in childhood; Eliza, who married Sam E. Johnson; Lucius Desha who was a West Texas ranchman; George Desha, who died in childhood, and James Monroe, a bachelor farmer, who died in Gillespie County, Texas at seventy-one. The eighth child, Kate, was born in Texas in 1861 and married Fannin Keele. In 1858, Mr. Bunton came to Texas following his brother, John Wheeler, Desha, and James Monroe, and his sisters, Caroline Quigley and Polly Kendall who had settled in Bastrop County much earlier. He located near Lockhart, Caldwell County, where he resided until the early 1880's when he and his wife moved to Stonewall, Gillespie County. He served four years in Captain Kelly's Company A and in Alexander Cowan's Company C, and, later, as Second Lieutenant in Major DeWitt Clinton's Battalion.

He was a large impressive man, standing six feet and three inches in height and weighing about two hundred and sixty pounds. His massive frame was well proportioned. He was a handsome man with fair skin, coal-black hair, and piercing black eyes. He was genial and hospitable, an excellent conversationalist, and greatly interested in government and politics. He died at Stonewall, August 22, 1895, and is buried at the cemetery at that place.

Priscilla Jane McIntosh

Priscilla Jane McIntosh was born July 8, 1821, in Russellville, Kentucky, the daughter of James William and Julia Ann (Miller) McIntosh.

The family was Scotch. Jane was a diminutive brunette, full of energy and vivacity, resourceful, practical, efficient and wise. She was quick of movement, patient, kind, and sympathetic in heart and manner. Her simple home was a favorite haven for her grandchildren when encouragement, comfort, or aid was needed. Her long life of nearly eighty-four years came to a peaceful end April 28, 1905 and she was laid to rest in the Johnson family cemetery near Stonewall.

Little is known of her early life or of her parents. She had a sister, Ella, and a sister, Rachel, who married William Radcliffe McIntire and reared three children, Holmes, Julia Ann, and John William in Saint Louis, Missouri. Descendants of Rachel live in Houston, Texas.

Reverend George W. Baines, Sr.

(Texas Historical and Biographical Magazine)

"I never knew a man more beloved and honored by the people he served."—Dr. F. Courtney, who knew him in Arkansas and Louisiana. "Fifty years is a long time to know a man without seeing something in him to condemn. A purer, better man never filled the various stations of life he was called to occupy."—L. N. Halbert, who was converted with him. "One of the best and most remarkable men I ever knew. Not a stain rests upon his name. It always seemed to me that he could see as far into the subject as it fell to the lot of man to do, and that he was wonderfully gifted in seeing the difficulties in the way of reaching correct conclusions. Fortunate was the young preacher who had him for counsellor when in deep theological waters, or in the midst of fiery trials. I never went to him without getting instruction and comfort."—M. V. Smith.

Reverend George W. Baines, Sr., born near Raleigh, North Carolina, December 29, 1809, was the eldest son of Rev. Thomas Baines, himself the son of Rev. George Bains, who came from Scotland, a Baptist preacher. The English style of spelling the name with an "e" was adopted by Thomas Baines. In 1817, the family moved to Georgia, and the next year to Alabama, near Tuscaloosa, where the subject of this sketch was reared on a farm, without education. After he became of age, by his own unaided efforts, first by cutting and rafting timber and afterwards by teaching school, he nearly finished the full course of study at the University of Alabama in Tuscaloosa. His health failing, during his senior year, 1836, he left school, but afterwards received the degree of A.M. from his Alma Mater. He is remembered by his college mate, Ex-Governor O. M. Roberts, as a modest, painstaking and hard-working student, and one who was greatly respected by all who knew him.

At the age of twenty-three, in a meeting conducted by the great revivalist, Reverend T. J. Fisher, some ten miles southwest of Tuscaloosa, during September, while engaged in teaching, he was converted, and was baptized by Rev. Robert Guthrie into Salem church, along with Reverends Halbert, Fox and White, and many others who did not become ministers. By order of the Philadelphia church, Tuscaloosa County, he was licensed to preach, July 20, 1834, at the age of twenty-five. Two years later, August 6, by order of Grant's Creek church, he was ordained, the sermon being preached by Rev. J. H. DeVotie, D.D., from 2 Timothy 4:5,6. Both his license and ordination papers bear the signature of his father.

A year later, 1837, on account of failing health (he was a lifelong dyspeptic), he went to Carroll County, Arkansas, in the hope of recuperating, and of planting churches in that wilderness country. For a year or two he held a commission from the Baptist Home Mission Society of New York City. In Arkansas he became widely known, and had great influence. At the earnest solicitation of his friends, he ran for the Fourth Legislature and was elected, his colleague being Robert Fancher, and the term lasting from November 7, 1842, to February 4, 1843. He spent seven years in Arkansas, during which he organized three churches and baptized one hundred and fifty people; and, when one remembers how sparsely the country was populated, and that he began at the beginning, the work appears a noble one indeed.

Influential as he afterwards was in Texas, it may be doubted that he had such influence as in Arkansas. The people were pioneers; he became one, and built his cabin in the forest. They were hunters, and took great pride in marksmanship and in their knowledge of game; he stood with the foremost in all these respects. It is not too much to say that, before his eye became dim, he was the surest rifle-shot at game and the closest at a mark, this writer ever knew. Whether the hunt was for turkey, deer, or bear, he seldom returned empty handed. The pioneers liked this in their preacher. Then, he took a wife from among them; lived as they lived; suffered their privations; and taught them faith, submission, love. He married Miss Melissa Ann, daughter of Nealy Butler, October, 1840. Her bridal tour was from her father's house to her husband's new cabin, and she rode behind him on the same horse. Ten children were born to them; four survive.

Some of the old settlers still remember the pioneer preacher, and he is pictured as a lithe, medium-sized man; having wonderful powers of endurance; with deep blue eyes and coal black hair; and they lovingly refer to him as "the best preacher that ever was in North Arkansas".

Yielding to conviction of duty, in 1844 he left Arkansas, and in July settled at Mt. Lebanon, Louisiana, where he remained six years. Soon he became known as the foremost preacher of any denomination in North Louisiana—so his old friends say. He preached at Mt. Lebanon, Minden, Saline, and one or two other points. Letters before me state that his influence was very great among the people, and that generally among the Baptists his counsel was law. He served the parish of Bienville as Superintendent of Schools for a while, and it is said that he could have had any office in the gift of the people. While living at Mt. Lebanon, he visited Texas, and assisted in the organization of the Baptist church at Marshall. He caught the Texas fever and had to come, although the strongest efforts were made to detain him in Louisiana.

In 1850, after a journey of seventeen days across the country, he arrived with his family, and Prof. Thomas George Edwards, a young Englishman, in Huntsville, Texas, where he located and served as pastor one year, during which time he won the lifelong friendship of the Maxcys, Wilsons and others, including General Sam Houston and his noble wife.

The Baptists of Texas immediately recognized his worth, and conferred on him almost every honor in their power. At the first session of the State Convention after he came to the State, he was elected Recording Secretary; appointed to preach on Sunday, although the meeting was in Huntsville; elected to represent the body in the Southern Baptist Convention; and was selected to preach the annual sermon for the next year. At this, his first meeting with the Convention, he reported on Home (State) Missions, and backed the report with a speech that made a profound impression. From that day to the close of his life, nobody ever doubted his interest in our State work; and from then to 1882, when he died, he was, in the language of the lamented Dr. W. C. Crane, "intimately connected with every good enterprise of the denomination". For thirty-two years his name is to be found in the minutes of the State Convention and of many Associations.

In 1851 the pastorate in Huntsville was given up for that at Independence, where he remained one year. In 1852 he moved to Anderson, where he labored as pastor and editor of the first Baptist paper in Texas, until 1861. Here his work was greatly blessed; the church flourished, being one of the largest, wealthiest and most intelligent in the State; the paper had a good circulation and was a controlling and educating force. The orthodoxy and ability of the editor were never questioned, among Baptists. General J. W. Barnes, of Anderson, who was intimate with the pastor and editor for very many years, rates him among the best and ablest men of the denomination; and he thinks that eternity will show the old Texas Baptist to have been the mightiest force for good, in Texas, up to the war, when it went down, of course.

In 1861, when the war with all its wrecks and griefs was upon us— when stout hearts faltered and wise heads were confused, the pastor-editor laid down the work he loved so well, and yielding to the call of his brethren, accepted the presidency of Baylor University at Independence. Those were trying times; but he managed to do a good work, and never once complained. For two years he struggled against fearful odds, and at last resigned on account of ruined health.

In January, 1864, we find him living on a farm, about two miles and a half west of Fairfield, Freestone County, and preaching to the churches at Fairfield, Springfield, Butler and another in the Cockrell neighborhood. While living in Freestone County he had the severest trials of his life; losing an old Negro who was greatly beloved, also his youngest child, Johnny Paxton Baines, and the precious wife, who for twenty-five years had been his chief earthly comfort, joy and support. Those were dark days; but nobody ever heard him murmur.

In the fall of 1866 he gave up his churches, and traveled until October of the next year, agent for the State Convention, and then settled at Salado, Bell County, as pastor there and of some other churches, including Florence in Williamson County. Bell County was his home until his death.

In 1877 he desired to retire for a time from active ministerial labor, especially as preachers were now more numerous than formerly, and as he was much interested in the matter of Baptist education in Texas. He therefore took an agency for the Educational Commission, believing that it promised most for Baptist education. Here, as always, he made himself felt, and did a noble work.

In 1881 the church of Salado would not hear a declination from him, and so he re-entered the pastorate there, giving his whole time to that work; and resigned, on account of feebleness of health, a short time before his fatal illness. After the death of his second wife, whom he married in Freestone County, he made his home with his daughter, Mrs. Annie Rosborough, in Belton. There he died, from malarial fever, December 28, 1882. He was buried in Salado; Rev. M. V. Smith conducting the funeral services. A very large concourse of friends were present to weep over one who was universally respected and loved.

From those who knew him best and loved him most, a few points have been gathered, and are here submitted to show what were his chief excellences.

General Barnes writes of him as a wonderfully clear thinker, and a most profound student on any matter his thought touched. He also refers to him as being exceedingly patient, and always well poised.

Old Brother Z. N. Morrell regarded him as a man whose staunchness and courage were never to be questioned; and he thought that Texas Baptists owe to him what they do not to any other man, for turning the popular tide of error in times of greatest peril, notably at Independence, in 1855.

Some who loved him long thought that his modesty was his greatest fault. He so loved a back seat. Others think his humility was beyond that of any person they ever knew. Brother M. V. Smith, who knew him as well as anybody, thinks that his love of peace among his brethren was his most prominent characteristic. All say that he was as perfect a type of the true Christian gentleman as they ever met. He was profoundly learned in the Bible, and it was his delight to open up the Scriptures to the ignorant and the wise. It required real temerity to challenge one of his teachings. The hymn he loved best is: "Alas! And Did My Savior Bleed!".

As a husband he was tender and loving; always considerate and solicitous. As a father he was firm, yet indulgent; insisting on strictest obedience, yet tenderly affectionate. There was no sacrifice he would not gladly have made for his wife or children. He loved his home; he was devoted to his family; he adored his God. "He rests from his labors, and his works do follow him."   —G. W. B.

The above is a copy from Texas Historical and Biographical Magazine, pages 480–485 inclusive, this day, August 16, 1932, in the Office of Records, Southwestern Baptist Theological Seminary.

                           Grace McFarland, Secretary of Records
Witness: Mrs. Wm. B. McGarity.

George W. Baines filled almost every position that a minister is called to occupy. He was first a pastor, then a missionary, editor of a Baptist paper, The Texas Baptist, the first of its kind in the State, for six years, agent for the State Convention, and agent for the Educational Commission. Having lived to a ripe old age, having cared tenderly for two Christian wives till death took them before him, having reared and educated five children, four of whom survive him and fill honorable positions in society, and having served the Baptist denomination faithfully for fifty years, his sun set without a cloud.

His life was pure and blameless. Not a shadow mars the beauty of his character. Gentle and quiet, soft in speech and modest in everything, he was yet a man of deepest convictions, and stood ever ready to defend them with a dauntless courage and forceful reasoning. His mind was exceptionally clear and logical. Always calm and selfpossessed, he never lost track of the subject under discussion, and no excitement could entangle him with side issues. If, in times of excited interest in public gatherings, the brethren became temporarily confused and likely to go wrong, the voice of this still and thoughtful man would never fail to make the needed correction. No man loved peace more dearly. He was distinguished as a peacemaker. His intimate acquaintance with the principles of church polity, and his love of peace and order in Zion made him a man of rare ability and value in the settlement of church troubles. He was a friend of missions and of learning, a lover of little children, a warm advocate of temperance, a genial companion, a wise counselor, a thorough and accomplished Bible scholar, a good writer and an able minister. His interest in young preachers was strong and tender. Patient and kind, he took special pleasure and pains to give them help, and rejoiced at their promise of usefulness. His path grew brighter to the end, and the memories of his unselfishness will not fade from those who knew and loved him even as the work he did will not cease to bear its golden fruitage.

—M. V. Smith

The Texas Baptist Herald—January 1883

Melissa Ann Butler

Melissa Ann Butler, the daughter of Nealy and Amy (Ozier) Butler, was born in North Carolina, June 2, 1824. While still a small child, she moved with her parents to Tennessee and within the next few years on to Carroll County, Arkansas where she was to reside until 1844. On October 20, 1840 she was married to Reverend George W. Baines, a Baptist pioneering preacher and educator. To them were born ten children, only five of whom reached maturity. From 1844 to 1850 the family lived in Mount Lebanon, Louisiana, moving on then to Huntsville, Texas. The lot of a minister's wife is seldom an easy one; Melissa's must have been particularly difficult, as her husband's duties required his absence from home much of the time, the care of the home and the children fell on her shoulders during these times; there were no conveniences in rural Texas at this period, but Melissa Ann did not falter, adapting herself to all emergencies with skill and grace. In 1861, she lost her brilliant first born, Thomas Nealy, the scholar and poet of her little flock, the young Confederate soldier dying in Virginia.

With this crushing sorrow and the increasing tensions of war days—two other sons soon joined the Confederate Army—Melissa Ann's days were filled with activities and anxieties. To her husband, her children, and her friends, she was a strength, a comfort, and an inspiration. Although her indomitable spirit was unconquered, her health was undermined and she fell ill and died January 21, 1865, at Fairfield, Texas. In a life span of little more than forty years, she had lived richly and well.

Melissa Ann (Butler) Baines was slender and fair, with a broad brow and beautiful brown eyes. Dr. Thomas George Edwards, who taught the Baines children in Louisiana and Texas, said of her: "She was a beautiful young woman with the whitest skin and the blackest hair I ever saw." She was modest and reserved, unselfish and devoted to her family. Her piety was equaled only by her courage.

John Smith Huffman, Jr.

John Smith Huffman, born in Bourbon County, Ky., May 7, 1824, was the son of John Smith and Suzanne (Ament) Huffman. He was an ambitious young man and soon left his father's farm to enroll in the University of Louisville's Medical School in 1841. In 1847 he came to Collin County, Texas as a Peters colonist, registering as a physician and taking up land from the Impresarios. In 1848, he married Mary Elizabeth Perrin, daughter of William and Dycea (Kerbey) Perrin, and they established a home near Rowlett in Collin County. The young couple prospered, enjoying a comfortable and happy home on their black land farm with fine cattle and one hundred blooded Kentucky mares. They had nine daughters and one son, all healthy, well-favored children. The war between the States brought great changes. As the war progressed, the young doctor enlisted in Captain Edward Chambers' Company D, 15th Battalion, Texas State Troops in July 1863. His letters from the battlefield reflect the deep concern he felt for his family, the great strain and suffering he felt as a surgeon ministering to the wounded soldiers, and his sorrow over the losing cause. He returned home at the close of the war completely broken in health with his nerves shattered. He died from the effects of the war June 22, 1865 at his home near Rowlett.

He was a handsome man of medium height with blue eyes and blonde hair, a pleasing personality, affable and agreeable in manner. Light-hearted and friendly, he was very popular. He felt a great sympathy for all human suffering and acute personal pain when unable to alleviate it. The cruel experiences of the war brought about the nervous breakdown which occasioned his death. He was buried in the Rowlett cemetery.

Mary Elizabeth Perrin

Mary Elizabeth Perrin, daughter of William and Dycea (Kerbey) Perrin, was born June 27, 1826 in Russellville, Kentucky. She was the fourth in a family of ten children: Abner, James, Catherine (Bryan), Mary Elizabeth, Ellen (Thomas), George, Charles, Amanda (Thomas), Anne, and William. All came to Texas with their parents in 1845 or 1846. William Perrin was a Peter's colonist and located on a grant of land in Collin County. Mary Elizabeth was a comely and industrious young woman, small in stature, with black eyes and hair. In 1848, she married young Dr. John S. Huffman, Jr., also a Peter's colonist with land near her father's. They made their home at Rowlett in Collin County, Texas.

Widowed in 1865, with ten children ranging in age from two to sixteen years, she undertook to carry on the farm. She was a woman of strong will, great determination, unbounded energy, and unusual housewifely skill. She lived to the advanced age of ninety, making her home during her last years with her youngest daughter, Lula, Mrs. Charles M. Largent, at Merkel, Texas. She was an omnivorous reader and a good conversationalist having retained all her faculties until her death, July 12, 1916.

Robert Holmes Bunton

Priscilla Jane (McIntosh) Bunton

Rev. George W. Baines Sr.

Baylor at Independence at the time
George W. Baines was its president
1861-62.

Melissa Ann (Butler) Baines and her daughter,
Annie Melissa.

John Smith Huffman Jr.

Lyndon Baines Johnson's
Early Ancestors

John Johnson

John Johnson was living in Oglethorpe County, Georgia in 1795. The records of Oglethorpe, Henry and Greene Counties, Georgia show John's residence in these counties until his death in March 1828. He was of English descent, but his residence before 1795 is unknown as is the name of his first wife, the mother of his six children. He married for the second time in Greene County, May 24, 1823 Joicy Bowdrie Fears, the widow of William Fears. She survived him and lived to an advanced age.

He participated in the land lottery of 1827 and was awarded 202½ acres in Lee County. His service in the Revolutionary War is recorded in the Survey Book and Grant Book in the Georgia State House.

Joseph Robert Bunton

Joseph Robert Bunton, born about 1782 in Rowan County, North Carolina, was the son of John and Mary (McClure) Buntin. He moved with his father to Sumner County, Tennessee before 1800. He engaged in farming in that section and in 1804, married Phoebe Ann Desha, the daughter of Robert and Elinor (Wheeler) Desha. They reared a family of eight children at the family home above Gallatin in Sumner County. There, in the early 1840's, Joseph Bunton passed away and was laid to rest in Gallatin, Tennessee.

Phoebe Ann Desha

Phoebe Ann Desha, the daughter of Robert and Elinor (Wheeler) Desha was born near the Kentucky border in 1784. She was among the youngest of twelve children. John, the eldest, was born in 1761; Joseph, born in 1768, was Congressman from Kentucky 1806–1819 and Governor of Kentucky from 1824 to 1828; Robert, born in 1777, was Congressman from Tennessee from 1827 to 1831; two brothers were killed by Indians in their youth; four sisters lived to maturity and marriage.

Phoebe Ann moved with her parents to Sumner County, Tennessee at an early age and there married Joseph Robert Bunton about 1802. She was a large, striking-looking woman with strong will and great ambition. She possessed all the fortitude and resourcefulness pioneering days required and implanted in her family of four stalwart sons and four daughters high ideals, perseverance, honesty and industry.

In the early days of the Texas republic she, having been left a widow, followed to Texas her two eldest sons, John Wheeler and Desha, and her daughters Caroline Quigley and Polly Kendall. Between 1850 and 1860, all of her sons settled in Hays and Caldwell Counties. Of the younger sons, Robert Holmes had removed from Logan County, Kentucky with his family in 1859 to Lockhart, Texas, and the other, James Monroe, settled in Hays County in 1854. Phoebe disposed of her property in Bastrop and made her home with her sons. A few years later she died at the home of her son, John Wheeler, at Mountain City, Hays County, Texas and was buried in the Robinson Cemetery near there.

Thomas Baines

Thomas Baines, the youngest son of George and Mary Baines, was born in Edenton, Chowan County, North Carolina, July 4, 1787. On February 13, 1808, he married in Perquiman County, North Carolina, Mary McCoy, a young Scotch girl, daughter of William and Julia McCoy. Thomas and an elder brother, James, were ordained as Baptist ministers in Clark County, Georgia, August 22, 1817. After about a year's residence in Georgia, the brothers and their families moved to Tuscaloosa, Alabama. Henry Foster in his "History of Tuscaloosa County Baptist Association" writes: "Thomas Baines was working in the churches of this county as early as 1818. He aided in constituting Bethel Church in 1818 and was for many years a member of that church. He was a member of a presbytery constituting Philadelphia, Friendship, and several other churches in this county. He was pastor of Ebenezer, (now First Baptist) at Tuscaloosa from 1822 to 1824. He was pastor of many rural churches and was very active in the churches of the Cahaba Association. He was the Moderator of the Convention of thirteen churches which met at Hopewell Church March 28, 1834 for the purpose of organizing an association, and was the Moderator of the Tuscaloosa Association which was organized by those churches on March 29, 1834. He wrote the "Circular Letter" on "Christian Unity". The reading of this letter would convince anyone that Mr. Baines was a man of deep spirituality and of incisive mentality. He was one of the strong preachers of his day, and was a power in shaping the policies of the Tuscaloosa Association.

In 1836, Thomas Baines moved to Mississippi where he died late in that year. The busy life of the pioneering preacher ended in less than fifty years. He was a serious, consecrated student, a tireless worker, an idealist, who translated his dreams into deeds. Three sons, the eldest a Baptist minister, a daughter, and his wife survived him. Thomas Baines changed the spelling of the family name from Bains to Baines.

Mary McCoy

In Perquiman County, North Carolina, in 1783, Mary McCoy was born, the youngest of the seven children of William and Julia McCoy. Her father was the son of the pioneer, James McCoy, who came from Scotland. William McCoy's will recorded March 18, 1795, in Perquiman County mentions his wife, Julia, and children: Joseph, Malita, James, Jonathan, Sarah, Elizabeth, and Mary. On February 13, 1808, Mary married young Thomas Bains. She went with her husband first to Georgia, then to Alabama and from there in 1835 to Mississippi. Following the death of Thomas Baines, she lived with her sons, first with the youngest, Joseph B. Baines in Harrison County, Arkansas, and later with the eldest, Rev. George W. Baines, at whose home in Fairfield, Texas, she died in 1864.

She was honored by all who knew her for her stern sense of duty, unfaltering courage, and practical wisdom.

Nealy Butler

Nealy Butler was born in North Carolina January 15, 1796. In early manhood, he married Amy Ogier and a few years later, moved to Tennessee where he resided for nearly ten years. About 1836, he removed with his family to Carroll County, Arkansas where he continued farming until shortly after the Civil War began. "A Reminiscent History of the Ozarks" thus explains his later movements. "Being substantially in favor of the Union of the States, Nealy Butler on the secession of Arkansas from the Union found it necessary for the protection of his life and property to migrate to the north which he did, locating in Stone County, Missouri where he made his home until his death in 1880; in which county his wife, Amy, also died a few years previously; both being quite aged."

He reared a large family, was an industrious, conscientious and God-fearing citizen, a man devoted to his family and loyal to his convictions and somewhat of an individualist.

Amy Ogier

Amy Ogier was born February 28, 1799, in North Carolina. She there married Nealy Butler, moved with him to Tennessee, Arkansas and finally to Stone County, Missouri where she died in about 1875. She had reared a family of ten children:

1. Wilson Butler, born in North Carolina 1820.
2. Martin Butler, Baptist minister.
3. Melissa Ann Butler, born 1824, North Carolina. Married Reverend George W. Baines; moved to Texas.
4. Tempie Butler, married Joe Dawson.
5. Elizabeth Butler, born 1828 in Tennessee; married Reverend James H. Paxton; moved to Texas.
6. John Butler, born 1831 in Tennessee.
7. Joel Ogier Butler, born 1834 in Tennessee.
8. William O. Butler, born 1838 in Arkansas.
9. Amy Butler, born in 1842 in Arkansas.
10. Nealy T. Butler, born in 1843 in Arkansas.

Amy Ogier was a descendant of the French Huguenot family of Louis and Catherine (Creuze) Ogier, silk merchants who came to Carolina with their nine children on the ship Union, in February, 1774. Louis

Ogier was descended from Pierre Ogier of France born in 1655. It is a long and illustrious line.

Three of the sons of Louis Ogier served with distinction in the Revolutionary War; they were George, Thomas, and Louis the second. This younger Louis was on the staff of Colonel Francis Marion, "The Swamp Fox". According to Fosdick's "French Blood in America": "After the fall of Charleston, Marion retreated to North Carolina where he found a number of his French countrymen which he organized into a corps which acquired the name of Marion's Brigade and its exploits were famous. For its chief officers Marion had ***** Captain Louis Ogier, the Postell brothers, all his bosom friends."

All Ogier descendants in America are descended from Louis, Thomas, or John Ogier, or their sister Charlotte (Ogier) Martin. Among the children of Louis and his wife Susan (Martin) Ogier were Louis, Susan, Charles, Martha, Jane, John Eliza and Amy.

John Smith Huffman

John Smith Huffman, born in Bourbon County, Kentucky, November 2, 1794, was the son of John Huffman and his wife, Catherine Lyter. He was married three times: first in 1818 to Suzanne Ament, by whom he had eight children; second to Lucinda Armstrong in 1831, by whom he had five children, and lastly in about 1844 to Helen Hall, a New England schoolteacher. In "The Lone Star State", Captain Benjamin Paddock refers to him in this wise: "John Huffman followed farming in Kentucky successfully until 1851, when he came to Texas and settled in Collin County. Here he spent the residue of his life and died at the advanced age of eighty-five. In Collin County he accumulated a large landed estate and for many years was largely interested in the stock business. He was the first to make a success of breeding short horn cattle in Texas, and he was also the first to introduce the Sir Archer breed of horses to the State. Indeed he was a man much in advance of his time, both in stock raising and farming, and he was well-known and highly respected all over the State."

John Huffman was of medium height, well-built, strong, very active and highly energetic. He rode his horse up until his death at eighty-five. Mentally alert, keenly interested in State and National affairs, he was an excellent conversationalist, gregarious and sociable. He had a great sympathy for the poor and unfortunate and was well-known for his charity. His erect form, clear blue eyes, and thick white hair made him an attractive figure. He died at his home near Plano, October 7, 1880, and is buried in the Rowlett cemetery.

Suzanne Ament

Suzanne Ament, the daughter of Philip Ament, was born in 1801 in Bourbon County, Kentucky near the Fayette County line. She had four sisters; Polly, who married Henry Lyter, Sally, who also married a Lyter, Catherine, the wife of John Childers, also another sister, the wife of David Halderman, and two brothers, Henry and George Ament. This we learn from the will of Philip Ament, (1836) on record in Bourbon County. Her father, Philip Ament, was of French extraction and was a soldier in the Revolutionary War.

Suzanne Ament married in about 1816 or 1817, John Smith Huffman and resided in Bourbon County, Kentucky until her death in May, 1831. She was the mother of eight children, leaving twin daughters, Mary and Martha, only one year old at her death. The name of Ament appears several times in each generation of Huffmans succeeding the gentle Suzanne; the vivacious little French girl, a sprightly brunette, lives on in memory despite her brief span of thirty years.

Nathan Barnett

"Nathan Barnett was born in New Kent County, Virginia in 1729; died in Greene County, Georgia in 1798. Served as a Revolutionary soldier from Georgia in the Battle of Kettle Creek, February 14, 1779, under General Elijah Clarke. Was given a "Bounty Grant" of land for his services." (From "Bounty Grant" book at Atlanta, Georgia.) He married in 1757 in Virginia, Lucy Webb, born in Virginia in 1731. They came to Georgia in 1768 and settled on the Little Kioka Creek in St. Paul's Parish, Georgia. Among their children were:

1. Nathan Barnett, Jr., born 1759 in Virginia, a Revolutionary soldier.
2. Mial Barnett, born 1760 in Virginia, a Revolutionary soldier.
3. John Barnett, born 1762 in Virginia, a Revolutionary soldier.
4. Claiborne Barnett, born 1759 in Virginia, a Revolutionary soldier.
5. Leonard Barnett, born 1773. Lived in Greene County, Georgia in 1828.

The above is from McCall's Roster of the Revolutionary Soldiers in Georgia.

The register of Saint Peter's Parish, New Kent County, Virginia lists the following:

Rebecca Bishop Barnett, ye daughter of Nathan Barnett and Lucy Barnett was born March 10, 1757 and baptized April 17. Mary Duke Barnett, ye daughter of Nathan and Lucy Barnett born July 23, 1758 and baptized September 3.

Family records show the birth of a son, William Barnett, in 1771, and a daughter, Suzanna Barnett.

Lucy Webb

Lucy Webb was among the eldest of the ten children of John and Peggy Webb, and was born in Virginia in 1731. The will of her brother, William Webb, recorded in Elbert County, Georgia and probated in 1823, names four brothers: John, Austin, Claiborne and Pleasant, and sisters: Lucy, Mary, Suky, Sally, and Patsy.

In 1757, she married Nathan Barnett and moved in 1768 to Georgia with him. Four of her sons fought with their father in the Revolutionary War. A fifth son, Leonard, was too young to fight. She also had daughters, Rebecca, Mary, and Susanna Barnett. Lucy lived in Greene and Elbert Counties in Georgia and died in 1808.

John Buntin II

John Buntin II was the son of John Buntine I, emigrant from Scotland. The date of his birth is unknown, but he, with his two brothers, Robert and James, and their father fought in the Revolutionary War. His mother had died when he was quite young. Leaving Rowan County, North Carolina, he came to Sumner County, Tennessee where he bought on January 4, 1800, 640 acres of land on Dry Fork or Bledsoe Creek. He and his wife, Mary (McClure) Buntin, had three children: William, who married Mary Cowan; Sarah, who married a Kerr; and Joseph Robert Buntin. His wife preceded him in death and he later remarried.

Robert Desha

Robert Desha was a descendant of the Huguenots of France, his father being one of that persecuted sect, who, in the middle of the seventeenth century, fled to America to escape the fury of intolerance, and to enjoy unmolested the religion of their choice. His father, the emigrant ancestor of the Deshas, settled in the Wyoming Valley, Pennsylvania. Robert was born about 1740 in Monroe County, Pennsylvania. About 1760, he married Eleanor Wheeler, daughter of Lt. Joseph (French and Indian War) and Maria (Holmes) Wheeler. In 1781, the Deshas emigrated to Kentucky, and in the following year, to the Cumberland District, Tennessee. They were the parents of twelve children, attained a position of influence and responsibility, and acquired considerable property. One son, Robert, was a Congressman from Tennessee; another, Joseph, became Congressman and Governor of Kentucky.

Robert Desha was a private in the Revolutionary War in 1780 in Tennessee troops under Captain John Boyles, and received a land grant of 640 acres near Bledsoe's Lick, Sumner County, Tennessee. There in the fall of 1816, following the passing of his wife, Eleanor, by several years, he died rich in years, experience, and wisdom. His will on file in Sumner County, Tennessee is most interesting and indicative of the leading traits of the great pioneer, Robert Desha.

John Buntine I

John Buntine I, emigrant from Scotland, came to Rowan County, North Carolina in 1758. There is in Salisbury, the county seat of Rowan County, the record of his purchase on January 19, 1762 of 640 acres.

At that time his wife had died, leaving three sons, John II, Robert, and James. All fought in the Revolution in which James was killed.

John Buntine finally dropped the "e" from his name. The spelling of the name was later to be changed from Buntin to Bunton.

John Buntine, first of the American Buntin's descended from a long line dating back to Finlay Bunting, who in 1398 received a grant of land in Dumbartonshire from Robert, the Third of Scotland, which he named Airdrock. The name of John was popular in the family. For several generations members of the Bunton family represented Dumbartonshire in the Scottish Parliament.

George Bains

George Bains was born January 26, 1741. He resided in Edenton, Chowan County, North Carolina. He may have been the emigrant ancestor of the Baines family, coming from Scotland as a youth, but it seems more plausible that he was a member of the Baines family of nearby Virginia and a descendant of the emigrant ancestor. He was a surveyor, as well as a planter, a man of education and ability. He meticulously recorded the birth of each of his eleven children, their marriages, the births of himself and his wife and their marriage date in county records; a practice most unusual for that time.

George Bains was called "Blackbeard" to distinguish him from others of the same name. From this, we infer that he had black hair, an identifying characteristic of the Baines family.

He had Revolutionary service and was a leader in his community. On May 28, 1769 he married Mary Creecy, born January 28, 1749, a daughter of Levi Creecy. Their marriage of thirty-three busy, fruitful, and happy years was terminated May 19, 1802 by the death of George. His life of little more than sixty years embodied the glorious heritage of his ancestry of Scottish kings and has been an inspiration to his American descendants.

WILL OF GEORGE BAINS

I, George Bains of the State of North Carolina and County of Chowan, being in a low state of health but of sound mind and memory, do this Seventh day of May, One Thousand Eight Hundred and Two make this my will in manner following, to-wit:

1st.   I give unto my beloved wife Mary the sum of twelve pounds to be paid annually by my executor out of the monies arising out of the sale of such property as may hereafter be appropriated by this instrument for that purpose.

2nd.   I give unto my son William Baines twenty five shillings.

3rd.   I give unto my daughter Catharine Johnson the sum of twenty five shillings.

4th.   I give unto my son George Baines twenty five shillings.

5th.   I give and bequeath unto my son John Baines and his heirs forever one hundred acres of land beginning at a water oak a corner of my land where I now live Patented by Col. James Blount thence down the Beachy Swamp running North 48 poles to a Bunch of Gums in the swamp still in the same course through the swamp to a persimmon on the North side of the swamp thence up the said swamp on the Northwest side to the crook thereof thence South 54½ W. to a line of marked trees that divides my property and Lovey Baines's thence along that line to a corner of maple trees in Blount's line thence down that line to the first station.

6th.   I give and bequeath unto James Baines my son and his heirs forever a certain piece or tract of land beginning in the swamp at a maple in George Bains line running North 65 West until a South course strike a gum that is Powells corner and mine s'd tract is to the Eastward of the red oak ridge thence along Powells line No. 60 W. 208 poles to Lemuel Standins corner thence along said Standins line No. 20 pole thence No. 40 W. 120 poles all my land lying to the Northward of the above mentioned lines to be the same more or less.

7th.   I give and bequeath unto my son Thomas Baines and his heirs forever a certain piece of tract of land beginning at a bunch of gums in the swamp at the mouth of the beachy branch thence running down the swamp No. 42½ E. to William Bains' corner thence up the William Baines line to the road thence up the road until it strikes Henderson Standins line thence along the said Standins line until it strikes Lovey Baines line thence along the said Lovey Baines line until it strikes John Baines line of the land before given in this instrument binding on the said John Baines line to the first station be the same more or less nevertheless.

It is my will if my said son Thomas should die before he arrives to the age of twenty-one years or have issue lawfully begotten of his body in that case it is my desire that the above recited land be equally divided between my son James and John and my daughter Sarah on the event of which taking place it is my will that the sum of fifty pounds be paid jointly between the said three children, that is to say, James, John and Sarah, to my daughter Catharine Johnson at any time in case she should become a widow and in no other case whatever. Also I give unto my said son Thomas Baines one large Church Bible, Dyches Dictionary, Sympsons Nited Elements, Adkinsons Epitomy on Navigation and the Mariners Compass rectified. Further it is my will and desire that my plantation heretofore given unto my son Thomas Baines be rented out to the best advantage at the discretion of my executors hereinafter mentioned for the use and support of my well beloved wife Mary, my son Thomas and my daughter Sarah, or the survivor of them until my son Thomas arrives to the age of twenty-one years.

Likewise it is my will and desire that my land not heretofore given away or mentioned on the North side of the Road between William Baines' land and Henderson Standins' land be sold by my hereinafter named executor on a credit of twelve months and the money arising from the sale of that with all my chattel property not heretofore given away be appropriated as follows:

First it is my desire that my executors as soon as the nature of the case will admit have all the brick work done to the house I now live in, that is to say, two brick chimneys and the house pillowed, also all the plank worked up that is now prepared to the best advantage in finishing at the discretion of my executors, the expense of which to be paid out of the money arising from the sale of the property above mentioned and the balance of the money remaining from such sale the one half of which is for the tuition and other expenses of my daughter, Sarah Baines, the other half for the tuition and other expenses of my son Thomas Baines after deduction out the sum of twelve pounds annually for the use of my wife as above stated.

I hereby nominate and appoint my friend Lemuel Creecy and my son James Baines executors of this my last will and testament. In witness whereof, I the said George Bains have hereunto set my hand and seal the day and year above written.

George Bains (seal).

Signed, sealed and delivered in presence of

Thomas Miers)
John Nixon)
Delight Burkett) Jurt.

The above foregoing will was proved in open Court at June Term 1802 by the oaths of John Nixon, Delight Burkett, two of the subscribing witnesses thereto at the same time James Baines, one of the executors therein named appeared and qualified as such by taking the necessary oaths.

James Norfleet, Clerk.

North Carolina, Chowan County

I, E. W. Spires, clerk Superior Court in and for the County and State aforesaid, do hereby certify the foregoing and attached TWO sheets to be a true copy as taken from and compared with the records in my office.

IN WITNESS WHEREOF, I have hereunto set my hand and affixed the official seal of office, this 4th day of January, 1946.

E. W. Spires
Clerk, Superior Court.

Declaration Signer

JOHN W. BUNTON

Portrait of John W. Bunton, signer of the Texas Declaration of Independence. This picture was given to the University of Texas library by Miss Brewie Bunton of Kyle, Texas, his granddaughter.

This same historian declares: "This committee was selected by a mass meeting of the settlers of Mina. There were a number of colonists who took part in this mass meeting who afterward became conspicuous in the affairs of the republic. Mr. Bunton was a

By LORENA DRUMMOND

Forming the nucleus for a noteworthy collection of pictures, possessions and personal documents of the signers of the Texas Declaration of Independence, Mrs. Mattie Austin Hatcher, archivist of the University of Texas, has secured a number of memorabilia of John W. Bunton who came to Texas from Tennessee in 1832, at the age of 25 years, and settled near his old friend, Edward Burleson, in what is now Bastrop County.

Among the effects of Mr. Bunton, all of which have come to the University library through the efforts of his granddaughter, Miss Brewie Bunton of Kyle, are his photograph, his cattle brand, the "Turkey Foot" brand, brands of brothers and those of several of his sons, and a letter written to him in 1837 by J. Pinckney Henderson, then a special agent and minister from Texas to the English and French courts.

Mr. Bunton was born, reared and educated in Tennessee. He belonged to the State militia of Tennessee and took an active part in the Indian fights on the Tennessee frontier. When he came to Texas he found the colonists needing men of his type to help combat the encroachments of Mexican tyranny. The first steps toward an independent organization in Texas were made through committees of safety, according to a sketch of Mr. Bunton by an historian dealing with the signers of the Declaration of Independence. Mr. Bunton was active in organizing one of the first of these committees, that at Mina, later known as Bastrop, in May, 1835, and was chosen as its first secretary.

man less than 30 years of age, strong and vigorous and filled with enthusiastic desire to render service to the country. He was a man of commanding personality, accustomed to hard and arduous...

Bunton Becomes Leader

"Mr. Bunton soon became prominently identified with the settlement and development of the country and joined in its defense against Indian raids. So active did he become in the country's defense that he was soon recognized as a leader in thought and action.

"When a consultation of all the people was called in 1835 to meet at San Felipe he was urged to permit the use of his name as a candidate to represent the municipality of Bastrop. He was elected by a large majority over two opponents. He attended the convention and joined in proclaiming a Declaration of Independence from Mexico and was a signer of that instrument. When a committee was formed to draft a constitution Mr. Bunton was appointed on that committee. He was appointed chairman of a special committee to report on the condition of the regular army.

"After the adjournment of the convention Mr. Bunton joined Company C, First Regiment Texas Volunteers, and participated in the Battle of San Jacinto. He made a record for bravery and daring in the precipitous charge against the Mexican breastworks. 'His towering form,' said Captain Billingsley, 'could be seen amidst the thickest of the fight. He penetrated so far in the ranks of the defenders of the breastworks that it is miraculous that he was not killed. But he came out of the deadly conflict unscathed.'

After Mr. Bunton's return to his home following the victory at San Jacinto he was elected a member of the First Congress of the Republic and was again chosen a member of the Third Congress. He died about 1872.

An illustrious descendant of John Buntine I, another John Bunton, was a Texas hero and statesman. He was Lyndon's great-uncle.

THOMAS BAINS
First Moderator—1834

Family Lines

[Editor's Note

This family genealogy was lovingly gathered by Mrs. Johnson from family Bibles, courthouse records, and tombstone dates.

Mrs. Johnson was an enthusiastic family chronicler but not a professional genealogist.]

Children of Sam Ealy (Jr.) and Rebekah (Baines) Johnson

1. Lyndon Baines Johnson, born Stonewall, Gillespie County, Texas, Thursday, August 27, 1908. Married San Antonio, Texas, November 17, 1934, Claudia Alta (Lady Bird) Taylor, daughter Thomas Jefferson and Minnie (Patillo) Taylor, born Karnack, Harrison County, Texas, December 22, 1912. They reside Stonewall, Texas. Their children are:
   a. Lynda Bird Johnson, born Washington, D.C., March 19, 1944.
   b. Lucy Baines Johnson, born Washington, D.C., July 2, 1947.
2. Rebekah Luruth Johnson, born Stonewall, Texas, September 12, 1910. Married Monterrey, Mexico, May 10, 1941, Oscar Price Bobbitt, son of Oscar Price and Maude (Wisner) Bobbitt. They reside 2403 Hartford Road, Austin, Texas. Their child is:
   a. Philip Chase Bobbitt, born Temple, Texas, July 22, 1948.
3. Josefa Hermine Johnson, born Stonewall, Texas, May 16, 1912. Married (1) Lake Charles, Louisiana, May 16, 1940, Lt. Col. Willard White; divorced, 1945; (2) Austin, Texas, April 23, 1955, James B. Moss. They reside Fredericksburg, Texas, and have one child, adopted:
   a. Rodney Moss, born Biloxi, Mississippi, April 14, 1948.
4. Sam Houston Johnson, born Johnson City, Texas, January 31, 1914. LL.B. Cumberland University, 1934, married (1) Mattoon, Illinois, December 28, 1940, Albertine Summers; divorced 1944. Married (2) Vera Cruz, Mexico, January 27, 1955, Mary Michelson Fish. They reside Austin, Texas. Two children by his first marriage are:
   a. Josefa Roxane Johnson, born Mattoon, Illinois, September 28, 1941.
   b. Sam Summers Johnson, born Austin, Texas, October 5, 1942.
5. Lucia Huffman Alexander, born Johnson City, Texas, June 20, 1916. Married Lockhart, Texas, September 18, 1933, Birge Davis Alexander. They reside in Johnson City, Texas, and have one child:
   a. Rebekah Sterling Alexander, born Fort Worth, Texas, February 13, 1944.

Bunton Line

I. JOHN BUNTINE I, married. Resided January, 1762, Rowan County, North Carolina. His children were:
II. JOHN BUNTIN II, died 1803, Sumner County, Tennessee. Married May McClure. Their children were:
   1. William Bunton, married Mary Cowan. Their son,
      a. John Bunton, born January 5, 1796; married December 22, 1819. His son:
         (1) William A. Bunton, born 1827. Married Jennie Irving Craighead. Their son:

III.

IV.

(a) William Allison Bunton, born 1877; married Elizabeth Sinclair.

2. Sarah Bunton, born 1780; married a Kerr; one son, John Kerr.

3. JOSEPH ROBERT BUNTON, born 1782, Rowan County, North Carolina. Married Phoebe Desha, born 1784, Logan County, Kentucky. Their children were:

1. Elizabeth Bunton, born 1805; married Nelson Bailey Turner. They had seven children: Joseph Desha Turner, John Wheeler Turner, Phoebe Ann Turner, Elizabeth Ellen Turner, Robert Bunton Turner, Mary A. Turner and James Nelson Turner.

2. John Wheeler Bunton, born February 22, 1807, Sumner County, Tennessee; died Mountain City, Hays County, Texas, August 23, 1879. Married Mary Howell. He served in the First and Third Congresses of Texas, having come to Texas in 1833. Was signer of Declaration of Independence of Texas. Took part in the storming of Bexar, and in Battle of San Jacinto; was one of the seven men who captured Santa Anna. He married Mary Howell in 1837. See chart.

3. Desha Bunton, born 1809; died   Married (1) Elizabeth Hudspeth; (2) Sallie Curry. Children were: John, born in 1837; Joel in 1842, and Robert in 1845.

4. Caroline Bunton, born in 1811. Married Colonel Quigley. Came to Texas in 1837. Had two daughters, Bettie, who drowned in Slaughter's Creek as a child, and 'Liza, who married Seth Mabry and had a daughter, Ellen.

5. Polly Bunton, born in 1813. Married John Kendall. Came to Bastrop, Texas in 1837.

6. Adelaide Bunton, born in 1815; died in Simpson County, Kentucky in 1846. She married George Harbison and had two children: Mary E. and Amos Kendall.

7. ROBERT HOLMES BUNTON, born September 7, 1818 in Sumner County, Tennessee; died at Stonewall, Texas, August 22, 1895. In 1840 he married Priscilla Jane McIntosh, who was born in Russellville, Kentucky, July 8, 1821, and died at Stonewall, Texas, April 28, 1905. Children on chart.

Children of John Wheeler and Mary Howell Bunton are:

1. Elizabeth Howell Bunton, born in 1838. Married at Cedar Creek, Texas, Dr. William Anderson Oatman, January 14, 1855. Children on chart.

2. Joseph Howell Bunton, born August 31, 1840. Married (1) Ann Miller; (2) Elizabeth Ford. Children were Henry and Marcus Bunton.

3. Thomas Howell Bunton, born December 25, 1842; died October 10, 1922. Bachelor.

4. Desha Bunton, born November 18, 1846; died December 21, 1925. Married Mary Manlove. Their children were: Mary Brewye Bunton, John Ashley Bunton, De Fla Bunton, Thomas Wilmot Bunton, William Manlove Bunton and Robert Desha Bunton. Children of John Ashley Bunton and William Manlove Bunton on charts.

5. William Howell Bunton, married Mary Robinson. Had two children: Willie, who died young, and Wendell Bunton.
6. James Howell Bunton, married Mary Taylor.

Children of Robert Holmes Bunton and Priscilla Jane (McIntosh) Bunton are:

1. Mollie Bunton, born Logan County, Kentucky; died in Caldwell County, Texas, about 1880. Married Matthew Copenhover.
2. Joseph Lloyd Bunton, born Logan County, Kentucky, September 13, 1844; died Austin, Texas, January 2, 1918. Married (1) Ella Everitt; (2) Lizzie Stillings. Children on chart.
3. John Desha Bunton, born 1846; died at about eight.
4. Eliza Bunton, born Russellville, Logan County, Kentucky, June 24, 1849; died Stonewall, Texas, January 31, 1917. Married Lockhart, Texas, 1867, Sam Ealy Johnson. Children on Johnson chart.
5. Lucius Desha Bunton, born Russellville, Logan County, Kentucky, August 22, 1853; died Shaffer, Texas, January 23, 1892. Married (1) Belle Jorah Porter; (2) Amy R. Lewis. Children on chart.
6. George Desha Bunton, born about 1854; died at age of eleven.
7. James Monroe Bunton, born Russellville, Kentucky, April 10, 1858; died Stonewall, Texas, February 8, 1929. Bachelor.
8. Kate Keele, born near Bastrop, Texas, January 3, 1861; died Fredericksburg, Texas, May 1, 1931. Married July 5, 1887, Fannin Keele. One child:
   (1) Oreale Ruth Keele, born August 2, 1888; married November 27, 1928, James W. Bailey.

Children of Dr. William Anderson and Elizabeth Howell (Bunton) Oatman:

1. John Bunton Oatman, born   ; died   . Married (1) Marie Saunders; (2) Marie O'Daniel. Children were:
   a. Hazel Oatman (Butler)
   b. Hermine Oatman (Reed)
   c. Adele Oatman (Wright)
   d. De Fla Oatman.
2. Jeneau Oatman
3. Mary Oatman, married (1) David Grossthwaite; (2) Wright.
4. Victor Oatman, born February 10, 1864; died December 23, 1927. Physician. Married Fannie May Sneed, born July 9, 1866 at Austin, Texas, September 27, 1888. Their children were:
1. Alice Lucile Oatman, born July 11, 1890. Married September 27, 1911, Joe W. Blakeslee and resides in Austin, Texas. Children are:
   a. Mary Frances Blakeslee, born November 24, 1913. Married J. Lyle Hamner, January 5, 1931, Austin, Texas. She has a daughter, Lyla Frances Hamner, born September 1, 1933.
   b. Joseph Travis Blakeslee, born October 5, 1919; married Gladys Youngblood, March 8, 1942. Their daughter,

Gladys Joanne Blakeslee, was born November 3, 1943.
    c. John Oatman Blakeslee, born October 14, 1922; married Georgia Bartosh, June 22, 1945.
2. Loda Alyne Oatman, born July 11, 1890; died March 2, 1891.
3. Bess Victorine Oatman, born January 10, 1892; married Tom Bird, December 27, 1920, at Austin, Texas. Their child is:
    a. Mary Elizabeth Bird, born October 14, 1922, married Dr. James R. Alexander, January 29, 1944. Their children are Mary Ann Alexander, born May 25, 1947 and James R. Alexander III, born July 16, 1952.
4. William Anderson Oatman, born May 27, 1893; married December 27, 1920, William R. Bird. Their son is:
    a. William R. Bird, Jr., born December 19, 1927; married Monette Standford, March 11, 1949. Child is Sandra Ann Bird, born March 26, 1952, Wichita Falls, Texas.
5. Sneed Travis Oatman, born March 6, 1898; died May 21, 1939. Married September 3, 1920, Dora Hicks.
6. Mary Elizabeth Oatman, born June 28, 1901; married September 25, 1921, Fred O. Clark. Resides New York. Children are:
    a. Barbara Clark, born September 27, 1925, who married Edward F. Denyer, February 7, 1949, and has one child, Laurie Denyer, born November 28, 1949.
    b. Fred O. Clark, born December 11, 1936.
7. John Bunton Oatman, born October 13, 1905; died May 21, 1939. Married April 19, 1924, Mae Ellis. Child is:
    a. Billie Bess Oatman, born August 26, 1925; married January 14, 1943, William G. Menefee. Children are Hazel Nan Menefee, born February 19, 1944 and Terry Ann Menefee, born July 6, 1951.
8. George Frank Oatman, born February 24, 1912; married May 8, 1936, Arline Book. Children are George Frank Oatman, Jr., born March 4, 1941 and Linda Kay Oatman, born August 10, 1944.

Johnson Line

I. JOHN JOHNSON, born March 28, 1764; died Oglethorpe County, Georgia, January 14, 1828. Married (1) Ann Ealy, born September 14, 1763; died Oglethorpe County, Georgia, January 15, 1815; (2) in Greene County, Georgia, May 24, 1823, Joicy (Bowdre) Fears. He was a Revolutionary soldier. Children:
1. Samuel Johnson, born November 16, 1788.
2. John Johnson, Jr., born August 13, 1790; died January 13, 1819. Married September 29, 1815, Nancy Williams. Children were Nancy, Polly and William Johnson.
3. Elizabeth Johnson, born October 10, 1792; died June 25, 1794.

4. Jesse Johnson, born April 28, 1795; died Lockhart, Texas, May 15, 1856. Married in Greene County, Georgia, November 14, 1817, Lucy Webb Barnett, born in Georgia, January 14, 1798; died Lockhart, Texas, March 13, 1857. Children on chart.
5. Mary (Polly) Johnson, born in Georgia, August 7, 1797; died Colorado Camp Post, Coleman County, Texas, January 9, 1886. Married Oglethorpe County, Georgia, July 4, 1797, Pleasant L. Barnett. Children on chart.
6. Richard Johnson, born in Georgia, August 25, 1800; died 1813.
7. Ann Johnson, born November 22, 1802. Married Henry County, Georgia, May 20, 1828, John C. Campbell.
8. Thomas J. Johnson, born in Georgia, April 10, 1808; died Bell County, Texas, November, 1895. Married (1) Elizabeth J. Johnson, born July 7, 1811; died December 22, 1830; (2) Mary Ann Echols, born April 16, 1813; died February 13, 1886. See chart.

II. JESSE JOHNSON, born Oglethorpe County, Georgia, April 28, 1795; died Lockhart, Caldwell County, Texas, May 15, 1856. Served as Sheriff of Henry County, Georgia, 1824–28. Came to Texas in 1846. Married November 14, 1817 in Greene County, Georgia, Lucy Webb Barnett, born January 14, 1798, Georgia; died March 13, 1817, Lockhart, Texas. She was the daughter of Leonard and Nancy Barnett. Their children were:

1. John Leonard Johnson, born October 28, 1818; died November 5, 1890. Physician and Baptist minister. Married: (1) Elizabeth Malone, born December 29, 1836; (2) Mary Carroll. See chart.
2. Nathan Barnett Johnson, born August 10, 1820; died before 1856. Married Elizabeth.
3. Ava Ann Johnson, born May 18, 1823. Married James Adams, Henry County, Georgia. Among children: Jesse, John, Thomas Adams.
4. Andrew Jackson Johnson, born January 27, 1825; died December 2, 1891. Married: (1) Mattie Tuttle; (2) Bettie Morris. See chart.
5. Amanda Melvina Johnson, born March 7, 1827. Married Manly Kelly.
6. Frances Washington Johnson, born May 5, 1829. Married Leonard Barnett. Their daughter, Lucy, married Miles Moore.
7. Mary Ann Elizabeth Johnson, born January 29, 1831; died February 11, 1897. Married Thomas Hunt. See chart.
8. Lucy Ann Johnson, born November 12, 1838; died February 25, 1915. Married McCarthy.
9. Jesse Thomas Johnson, born July 6, 1836; died March 12, 1877.

III. 10. SAMUEL EALY JOHNSON, born November 12, 1838, in Alabama; died February 25, 1915, at Stonewall, Texas. Married December 11, 1867 at Lockhart, Texas, Eliza Bunton, born June 24, 1849; died January 30, 1917. Their children were:

1. Mary Johnson, born Hays County, Texas, October 1, 1868; died El Paso, Texas, April 18, 1909. Music teacher. Married Ed Walling in 1888.
2. Frank Barnett Johnson, born August 1, 1870, Buda, Texas. Married 1892, Clarence Martin. One child:
   a. Thomas Johnson Martin, born March 10, 1894, Kerrville, Texas; died September 21, 1948, Fredericksburg, Texas. Lawyer and State Representative. Married (1) Olga Priess, Fredericksburg, Texas, March 10, 1915, divorced; (2) Lela Black, 1929. A son,

Clarence (Nookie) Martin, was born April 1, 1916. An engineer, living in Los Angeles, California. Married Dorothy Thomas. They have two children:
1. Sandra Thomas Martin, born April 20, 1945.
2. Tom Johnson Martin, born December, 1947.
3. Ava Johnson, born October 18, 1872; died Blanco, Texas, March 11, 1955. Teacher. Married John Harvey Bright, teacher, August 19, 1906. Children:
   a. Mary Eliza Bright, born July 21, 1907. Married Dick Allison. Resides in Houston, Texas. Teacher.
   b. John Harvey Bright, Jr., born March 22, 1910. Engineer. Married Hattie. Children are:
      1. Beverly Elaine Bright, born November 10, 1939.
      2. John Harvey Bright III, born October 17, 1943.
   c. Dorothea (Baby Sue) Bright, born May 9, 1912. Married (1) Jack Watson, divorced; (2) Chetwood Askew. Children are:
      1. Robert Gordon Askew, born July 2, 1943.
      2. Lauren Sue Askew, born May 9, 1948.
      3. Ava Allison Askew, born November 20, 1954.
4. Lucie Johnson, born Buda, Texas, July 1, 1875; died Austin, Texas, August 8, 1950. Married Stonewall, Texas, James Sterling Price (1874-1948).
5. Sam Ealy Johnson, Jr., born Buda, Hays County, Texas, October 11, 1877; died Austin, Texas, October 23, 1937. Married Fredericksburg, Texas, August 27, 1907, Rebekah Baines. (Children on chart)
6. Thomas Jesse Johnson, born Buda, Texas, May 24, 1880; died January 2, 1952. Married Kittie Chapman in 1904. Children are:
   a. Ava Johnson, born August 2, 1905. Teacher. Married October 16, 1923, Ohlen Cox. One child:
      1. William Jay (Corky) Cox, born Johnson City, Texas, August 9, 1929. Teacher. Married Leatrice Garrison. Children:
         a. Deborah Jay Cox, born January 15, 1951.
         b. Thomas David Cox, born October 18, 1953.
   b. Margaret Johnson, born May 1907. Married Henry Kimball, January 1, 1929. One child:
      1. Margaret Ann Kimball, born September 21, 1930.
   c. James Ealy Johnson, born November 29, 1909. Rancher. Married (1) Louise Black; (2) Naomi Davis.
7. George Desha Johnson, born Buda, Texas, January 7, 1883; died Houston, Texas, March 11, 1940. Graduated 1915 University of Michigan. Taught in public schools of Texas many years. Head of History Department, Sam Houston High School, Houston.
8. Kate Johnson, born Buda, Texas, July 21, 1885; died Austin, Texas, 1934. Married (1) Tom Odiorne, September, 1907; (2) Turner Martin.
9. Jessie Hermine Johnson, born Buda, Texas, May 6, 1883. Married Silas Hatcher. Resides in San Saba, Texas. One child:
   a. Eliza Ruth Hatcher, born September 13, 1915. Married December 27, 1945, Austin, Texas, Eldon Booker. Children are:

1. George Thomas Booker, born January 21, 1948.
2. Eldon Wesley Booker, born January 25, 1951.

Baines Line

GEORGE BAINS, planter, surveyor, service in American Revolution. Born January 26, 1741; died Edenton, Chowan County, North Carolina, May 19, 1802. Married May 28, 1769, Mary Creecy, born January 28, 1749, daughter Levi Creecy, Jr. Their children were:

1. William Bains, born March 13, 1770; married February 20, 1797, Hannah Burkett, daughter, Thomas Burkett. A daughter:
   (1) Sarah Burkett, born November 19, 1797; died April 26, 1798.
2. Catherine (Catcy) Bains, born January 6, 1772; married February 1, 1791, Joshua Johnson. Children:
   (1) Mary Johnson, born February 21, 1792.
   (2) Charles Johnson, born May 1, 1793; died November 12, 1794.
3. George Bains, born May 1, 1773; married August 21, 1796, Rachel Branch, daughter Isaiah Branch.
4. Mary Bains, born April 12, 1775. Married King Luten, December 5, 1793; died March 20, 1795.
5. John Bains, born January 4, 1777; married Elizabeth Scott, October 29, 1803.
6. James Bains, born December 22, 1778. Married Catherine Powell, September 21, 1805; died Alabama 1836. Baptist minister.
7. Charles Bains, born January 13, 1781; died October 26, 1784.
8. Isaac Bains, born December 20, 1782; died September 26, 1800.
9. Cornelius Bains, born June 18, 1785; died December 19, 1794.
11. Sarah Bains, born February 24, 1790.
10. THOMAS BAINS, born July 4, 1787; died in Mississippi, December, 1836. Baptist minister. Married February 13, 1808 in Perquiman County, North Carolina, Mary McCoy, born North Carolina, 1794; died Fairfield, Texas, 18??, daughter of William and Julia McCoy. Scotch descent. Their children were:

   1. GEORGE WASHINGTON BAINS, born December 29, 1809, Perquiman County, North Carolina; died December 28, 1882, Belton, Texas. Editor, Baptist minister, educator. Married (1) October 20, 1840, Carroll County, Arkansas, Melissa Ann Butler, born North Carolina, June 2, 1824; died Fairfield, Texas, January 21, 1865. She was daughter of Nealy and Amy Ogier Butler. Married (2) Cynthia Williams. Children of George W. and Melissa Ann were:

      1. Thomas Nealy Baines, born Carroll County, Arkansas, August 20, 1841; died November 7, 1861, in Captain John William Hutchinson's Co. of Greys, 17th Brigade, C.S.A.
      2. William Martin Bains, born Carroll County, Arkansas, November 17, 1842; died May 1, 1912, San Diego, California. Service in C.S.A. Married (1) September 13, 1865, Rockdale, Texas, Sarah Elizabeth Owen, born January 31, 1846; died April 15, 1867, daughter of John H. and Elizabeth G. Owen. Married (2) September 29, 1868,

Navasota, Texas, Elizabeth Virginia Terrell, born 1848, Newman, Georgia; died San Diego, California, May 1, 1929, daughter of Dr. Joel W. and Elizabeth Wingfield Terrell. Children of William M. Bains on chart.

3. Mary Elizabeth Baines, born January 13, 1845; died in infancy.
4. JOSEPH WILSON BAINES, born Mount Lebanon, Louisiana, January 24, 1846; died Fredericksburg, Texas, November 18, 1906. Teacher, editor, lawyer; in Confederate service. Married September 12, 1869, Rowlett, Collin County, Texas, Ruth Ament Huffman, born Collin County, Texas, December 10, 1854; died San Antonio, Texas, February 13, 1936; daughter of Dr. John Smith and Mary Perrin Huffman. Children on chart.
5. George Washington Baines II, born September 8, 1848, Mount Lebanon, Louisiana; died Fort Worth, Texas, March 23, 1923. Baptist minister and educator. Married (1) September 8, 1875, Burleson County, Texas, Cornelia Holmes, born September 14, 1854; died Rockdale, Texas, October 22, 1880. Married (2) Calvert, Texas, November 1, 1882, Annie McIntosh, born October 29, 1854, Sunderland, England; died Mansfield, Texas, May, 1949. Children of George W. Baines II on chart.
6. James O'Neal Baines, born December 19, 1852; died in infancy.
7. Annie Melissa Baines, born January 24, 1854, Anderson, Texas; died Belton, Texas, June 17, 1897. Married Salado, Texas, June 5, 1878, William Edwin Rosborough, lawyer, born July 18, 1847, Tennessee; died Belton, Texas, January 28, 1926. Children:
    (1) George David Baines Rosborough, Belton, Texas. Writer. Born March 15, 1879; died March 7, 1943.
    (2) William Edwin Baines, died in infancy.
8. Taliaferro Baines, born Anderson, Texas, July 1, 1859; died Salado, Texas, June 5, 1870.
9. Johnnie Paxton Baines, born March 29, 1863; died Fairfield, Texas, May, 1865.

2. Julia Ann Baines, born in North Carolina, 1812; died Carthage, Texas, 1855. Married in Alabama, 1832, Abraham Marshall Hill, born 1812; died 1865. Their children were:
    1. Thomas B. Hill, born Mississippi, March 10, 1834; died in Confederate service. Married; no children.
    2. Mary A. Hill, born Mississippi, December 31, 1836; married Wilson Anderson. They had two children: William and Mollie.
    3. James T. Hill, born July 31, 1838; married (1) Sarah Womack; (2) Mary Ann Womack. Doctor.
    4. George M. Hill, born Arkansas, October 25, 1840; died Civil War. Bachelor.
    5. Andrew W. Hill, born Arkansas, May 6, 1843; married Lila Watson.
    6. Sarah Frances Hill, born Arkansas, August 10, 1845; died in childhood.
    7. Margaret G. Hill, born Arkansas, January 13, 1848; married Thomas McClendon.
    8. Julia McCoy Hill, born Carthage, Texas, January 5, 1851; died

Lufkin, Texas, November 21, 1932. Married August 4, 1869, Robert L. Longino. Children on chart.

    9. Abraham Marshall Hill, born Carthage, Texas, February 20, 1854.

3. William C. Baines, born March 9, 1814, in North Carolina; died in San Bernadino, California, April 1, 1895. Married in 1837, Catherine Turner in Alabama, his brother, George W. Baines, officiating. Came to Texas about 1840. Merchant and cattleman. Children of William C. and Catherine Baines were:

    1. Charles Silas Baines, born in Alabama, March 9, 1839; died Denton, Texas, September 25, 1910. Married (1) Harriet Hoffman, who died 1868; (2) Augusta Bryan, born October 16, 1847; died January 9, 1937. Children of Charles Silas Baines on chart.

    2. Mary Elizabeth Baines, born Texas, August 24, 1841; died June 2, 1894.

    3. Robert Thomas Baines, born Texas, April 10, 1844; married Sabina Perrin.

    4. Nancy Sophronia Baines, born Texas, August 24, 1846.

    5. William George Baines, born Texas, June 30, 1849.

    6. Martha Julia Baines, born Texas, September 16, 1851.

II.   7. James Henry Baines, born Texas, December 10, 1853; died June 26, 1920. Married Cora A. McLemore. Children on chart.

    8. John M. Baines, born Texas, 1855; died in childhood.

    9. Joseph Groves Baines, born Texas, May 3, 1859.

V.   10. Edwin Porter (Doc) Baines, born Texas, August 9, 1861; died Novice, Texas, 1932. Married (1) Mary Bryan; (2) Ora May Freeman; (3) Nellie Pauline King. Children on chart.

4. Joseph Benjamin Baines, born Tuscaloosa, Alabama, September 27, 1820; died Oklahoma City, Oklahoma, December 4, 1904. Married in Carroll County, Arkansas, January 1, 1840; Hannah Frances Beller, born Huntsville, Alabama, December 29, 1822; died Oklahoma City, Oklahoma, 1912. Their children were:

    1. Thomas Baines, born Arkansas, 1841. Physician. Married French woman. They had three sons: (1) Schwartz, a doctor; (2) Ned; (3) Faust, a minister, and a daughter, Ida.

    2. Mary Matilda Baines, born Carroll County, Arkansas, January 14, 1842; died Austin, Texas, February 16, 1927. Married April 3, 1864, Joseph M. Bailey, born Tennessee, January 29, 1841; died Gatesville, Texas, June 5, 1939. Children on chart.

    3. Benjamin Baines, born Arkansas, about 1845. Physician. Married and had one son, Benny, a preacher in Texas.

    4. George M. Baines, born April 3, 1848; died October 7, 1935. Married Gatesville, Texas, May Scott Winfrey. Lawyer; resided Texas and Arkansas. Children on chart.

    5. Joshua Irving Baines, born July 4, 1851; died in Arkansas. Teacher. Married October 31, 1880, Tennessee, Ocie Wright. Children on chart.

    6. Pinkie Baines, born in 1853. Teacher. Married John Sanders, a business man; had one son, who died early.

    7. Anna Baines, born in 1855; married Bill Smith. Had a son, Joe, and a daughter, Blountie.

8. McCoy Baines, born in 1857. Teacher. Married; had three sons: Pink, France, and Marshall, and two daughters.
9. David Baines, born in 1859. Doctor. Married; had one son.
10. Blount Baines, born in 1861, bachelor, tavern keeper. Resided Oklahoma City, Oklahoma.

William Martin Baines

William Martin Baines, born Carroll County, Arkansas, November 17, 1842; died San Diego, California, May 1, 1912. Service in C.S.A. Married (1) Sarah Elizabeth Owen, September 13, 1865, Rockdale, Texas; (2) Elizabeth Virginia Terrell, September 29, 1868. Children were:
1. Myra Fleming Baines, born Rockdale, Texas, February 21, 1867; died September 15, 1928. Married Navasota, Texas, September, 1886, Joseph Henry Hearn. Children were:
   a. Edna Ernestine Hearn, born Navasota, Texas, January 21, 1888; died February 15, 1937. Married Grover Stanfield Thompson, June 20, 1910. One son:
      (1) Henry Durward Thompson, born March 10, 1910; married December 25, 1936, Freddie Marriner. Their children are:
         (a) Henry Durward Thompson, Jr., born November 1, 1937.
         (b) Richard Standfield Thompson, born July 28, 1948.
         (c) Gregory Marriner Thompson, born June 26, 1950.
   b. Johnnie Myrle Hearn, born March 15, 1893, Beeville, Texas. Married May 28, 1938, George Fahr, Beeville, Texas.
2. Martha Elizabeth Baines, born Rockdale, Texas, 1870; died Beeville, Texas, June, 1848. Married Harvey C. Stiles, horticulturist. Their children were:
   a. Roger Stiles, farmer, near Beeville; twice married. Several children.
   b. Robert Stiles, advertising executive; twice married. Resides San Antonio.
   c. John Stiles.
   d. Edwin Stiles, died young.
   e. Dorothy Stiles.
   f. David Stiles, lawyer and promoter. Married Benna _____; resides Victoria, Texas. Has one son.

Joseph Wilson Baines

JOSEPH WILSON BAINES, born January 24, 1846, Mount Lebanon, Bienville Parish, Louisiana; died November 18, 1906, Fredericksburg, Gillespie County, Texas. Editor, teacher, lawyer. Married September 12, 1869; Rowlett, Collin County, Texas, Ruth Ament Huffman, born Rowlett, Texas, December 10, 1854; died February 13, 1936, San Antonio, Bexar County, Texas. She was the fifth child of Dr. John Smith and Mary Elizabeth Perrin Huffman. Children are:
1. REBEKAH BAINES, born June 26, 1881, McKinney, Collin County, Texas; resides Austin, Texas. Married August 20, 1907, Fredericksburg, Gillespie

County, Texas, Sam Ealy Johnson, Jr., born October 11, 1877, Buda, Texas; died October 22, 1937, Austin, Texas. Farmer, teacher, stockman, realtor, State Representative. Eldest son of Sam Ealy and Eliza Bunton Johnson. She resides 2519 Harris Boulevard, Austin, Texas. Children are:

(a) Lyndon Baines Johnson, born August 27, 1908, Stonewall, Gillespie County, Texas; married San Antonio, Texas, November 17, 1934, Claudia Alta (Lady Bird) Taylor, daughter Thomas Jefferson and Minnie Taylor, Karnack, Texas. Teacher, secretary, State Director, N.Y.A., Congressman 10th, Texas District, Senior U.S. Senator, ranchman. Resides Stonewall and Johnson City, Texas and Washington, D.C. Children are:

(1) Lynda Bird Johnson, born Washington, D.C., March 19, 1944.
(2) Lucy Baines Johnson, born Washington, D.C., July 2, 1947.

(b) Rebekah Luruth Johnson, born September 12, 1910, Stonewall, Gillespie County, Texas. Teacher, worked Library of Congress several years. Married May 10, 1941, Monterrey, Mexico, Oscar Price Bobbitt, advertising manager KTBC radio and T.V. Station, Austin, Texas. One child:

(1) Philip Chase Bobbitt, born July 22, 1948, Temple, Texas.

(c) Josefa Hermine Johnson, born May 16, 1912, Stonewall, Gillespie County, Texas. Teacher, secretary. Married May 16, 1940, Lake Charles, Louisiana, Lt. Com. Willard White; divorced. One child:

(1) Rodney White, adopted, born April 14, 1948, Biloxi, Mississippi.

(d) Sam Houston Johnson, born January 31, 1914, Johnson City, Blanco County, Texas. Public relations. Has law degree. Married, Mattoon, Illinois, December 28, 1940, Albertine Sommers; divorced 1945. Children:

(1) Josefa Roxane Johnson, born September 29, 1941.
(2) Sam Summers Johnson, born October 5, 1942.

(e) Lucia Huffman Johnson, born June 20, 1916, Johnson City, Blanco County, Texas. Married September 18, 1933, Lockhart, Caldwell County, Texas, Birge Davis Alexander; teacher, construction engineer C.A.A. They reside Johnson City, Texas. One child:

(1) Rebekah Sterling Alexander, born February 13, 1944, Fort Worth, Texas.

2. Huffman Baines, born April 7, 1884, Austin, Travis County, Texas. Electrical engineer, traffic chief Southwestern Bell Telephone Company. Married (1) June 19, 1908, Wharton, Texas, Dora Marsh, born June 19, 1889, London, England; died August 11, 1941, San Antonio, Texas. Married (2) 1942, San Antonio, Texas, Ovilea Cook Bogard. One child of first marriage:

(a) Huffman Baines, Jr., born August 5, 1918, Austin, Texas. Insurance agent. Married September 20, 1941, Winnie Jo Handy, born October 28, 1920, daughter of Kenneth Lee and Annie Cook Handy of Kenedy, Texas. The Huffman Baines family reside 3314 Perry Lane, Austin, Texas. Children are:

(1) Marsha Baines, born August 20, 1942.
(2) Annette Baines, born January 11, 1946, Austin, Texas.

3. Josefa Baines, born May 21, 1889, Blanco, Blanco County, Texas. Married May 21, 1908, San Marcos, Texas, Dr. William Edgar Saunders, dentist, born September 26, 1883, Wimberley, Texas; died March 9, 1947, San Antonio, Texas. She resides 427 Fulton Avenue, San Antonio, Texas. Children are:

(a) Ruth Josefa Saunders, born June 3, 1910, San Marcos, Texas. Married May 14, 1932, San Antonio, Texas, Oscar Deweese, realtor, born July 31, 1908, San Antonio, Texas. They reside Hollywood, California and have one child:
    (1) Diana Deweese, born August 1, 1934, Hollywood, California.
(b) Margaret Virginia Saunders, born May 10, 1915, San Marcos, Texas. Married December 19, 1936, San Antonio, Texas, Major Paul Kinnison, instructor Y. S. A. Children are:
    (1) Paul Kinnison, Jr., born June 3, 1938, San Antonio, Texas.
    (2) Karen Kinnison, born February 10, 1940, San Antonio, Texas.
    (3) William Edgar Saunders, born June 10, 1943, San Antonio, Texas.

George Washington Baines II

George Washington Baines II, born Mount Lebanon, Bienville Parish, Louisiana, September 8, 1848; died Fort Worth, Tarrant County, Texas, March 3, 1923. Baptist minister and educator. Married (1) Burleson County, Texas, September 8, 1875, Cornelia Holmes, born September 14, 1854; died Rockdale, Texas, October 22, 1880. Married (2) Calvert, Texas, November 1, 1882; Annie McIntosh, born Sunderland, England, October 29, 1854; died Mansfield, Texas, May 1949. Children of George W. and Cornelia Holmes Baines were:

1. George Oliver Baines, born Rockdale, Texas, December 4, 1876; died December 4, 1876.
2. Horton Trueheart Baines, born Rockdale, Texas, April 10, 1878; died November 3, 1878.
3. Cornelia Holmes Baines, born Rockdale, Texas, October 7, 1880; died Temple, Texas, December 4, 1916. Married San Marcos, Texas, 1910, Weir L. Matthews, born June 15, 1879; died September 24, 1924.

Children of George W. and Annie McIntosh Baines were:

1. George Washington Baines III, born El Paso, Texas, December 2, 1883; banker, realtor. Married Alpine, Texas, December 31, 1908, Maude Hancock, born October 16, 1887, daughter William Box and Nellie Powe Hancock. Their children:
    a. Dorothy Baines, born Alpine, Texas, June 28, 1910; died July 22, 1911.
    b. Helen Baines, born Alpine, Texas, March 21, 1912; died Dallas, Texas, May 21, 1937. Married Alpine, Texas, December 26, 1935, Brice Childress Moore, born August 15, 1907. She held B.A. degree Sul Ross College; art student.
    c. Elizabeth Baines, born Alpine, Texas, March 25, 1915. Married Monterrey, Mexico, April 3, 1940, Edwin Mackey Elliott, advertising agent, born December 13, 1910. Reside at Los Angeles, California. She is teacher with B. A. degree from Sul Ross College; M. A. University of Texas. Children are:
        (1) Randall Baines Elliott, born Los Angeles, California, August 2, 1941.
        (2) George Edwin Elliott, born Los Angeles, California, December 16, 1942.

2. William McIntosh Baines, born El Paso, Texas, October 24, 1885; married Alpine, Texas, June 28, 1911, Ruth Weakley, born Tokeen, Texas, September 28, 1889. Traveling salesman. Children:
   a. William McIntosh Baines, Jr., born San Antonio, Texas, September 25, 1914; died January 17, 1917.
   b. Ruth Baines, born San Antonio, Texas, July 19, 1916. Married Washington, D.C. March 20, 1938, William Woodrow Bain, born August 15, 1914, Stockdale, Texas, banker. They reside Devine, Texas. Children:
      (1) William Howard Bain, born October 11, 1940; died San Antonio, Texas, September 11, 1941.
      (2) Bonnie Louise Bain, born December 19, 1942.
      (3) Thada Marie Bain, born May 1, 1945.
   c. John Collier Baines, born San Antonio, Texas, December 21, 1921; died Dallas, Texas, May 3, 1944.
3. Janet Baines, born El Paso, Texas, November 22, 1888. Married San Marcos, Texas, July 5, 1911, Ernest Delwin Brockett. Jeweler and farmer, born Macon County, Tennessee, March 11, 1879. She is a teacher, with B. A. degree from Baylor University. They reside at Mansfield, Texas. Children are:
   a. Ernest Delwin Brockett, Jr., born Itasca, Texas, April 16, 1913. Engineer for Gulf Oil Corporation. Married Fort Worth, Texas, March 7, 1936, Frances Maxine Sammons, born February 17, 1914, Mathis, Texas. They reside Caracas, Venezuela. Children are:
      (1) Belmont Sammons Brockett, born Odessa, Texas, July 24, 1937. Student.
      (2) Janet Brockett, born July 15, 1951.
   b. Genevieve Brockett, born Fort Worth, Texas, June 22, 1921. Married March 15, 1944, John McCarroll, Jr., chemist. Children are:
      (1) John McCarroll III, born October 28, 1946.
      (2) James Ernest McCarroll, born September 5, 1949.
4. Annie Baines, born Weatherford, Texas, July 3, 1891; died Gatesville, Texas, March 22, 1948. Married San Marcos, Texas, June 12, 1919, John P. Reesing, druggist, born Waco, Texas, October 4, 1887. She received B. A. degree Baylor University, 1913 and taught fifteen years. Children are:
   a. John Palmer Reesing, Jr. born Gatesville, Texas, September 15, 1920. Teacher with degree B. A. Baylor University 1941; M. A. Tulane 1942, and Ph. D. Harvard, 1954. Instructor Oberlin College, Oberlin, Ohio.
   b. Frances Louise Reesing, born Gatesville, Texas, April 9, 1924, B. A. degree Baylor University, 1946. Married Gatesville, Texas, June 12, 1948, Rembert H. Wooldridge Jr., druggist, Midland, Texas.

Huffman Line

JOHN PETER HOFFMAN, born in Germany; died Baltimore, Maryland, 1748, wife, Appolonia, was executor of his estate. His son:
JOHN HOFFMAN, born 1728; died 1802, Culpeper, Virginia. Married Catherine, Hagerstown, Maryland, 1768. Served in American Revolution, 7th, 11th, and 15th Virginia Regiments under Capt. John Roberts and Lt. Col. John Cropper.

1. JOHN HOFFMAN, born Bourbon County, Kentucky, May 31, 1766; died in Missouri, July 23, 1826. Married in 1790 Catherine Lyter, born May 1, 1771; died December 15, 1831.
2. Catherine Hoffman,
3. Susanna Hoffman, born in Bourbon County, Kentucky; married Henry Siebert.
4. Michael Hoffman, born 1776; died 1827; married Mollie Hirschman.

The children of John and Catherine (Lyter) Hoffman were:

1. Philip Hoffman, born 1792; died young.
2. JOHN SMITH HUFFMAN, born November 2, 1794, Bourbon County, Kentucky; died October 7, 1880, Collin County, Texas. Married (1) Suzanne Ament, born 1800; died 1831; (2) Lucinda Armstrong, born 1804; died 1842; (3) Helen Hall, born 1829.
3. Joseph Huffman, born in Bourbon County, Kentucky, August 19, 1797; died May 20, 1854. Married November 25, 1824, Catherine Smeltzer, born November 12, 1804; died April 2, 1852.
4. Michael Huffman, born Bourbon County, Kentucky, 1800; died Dallas County, Texas, 1860. Married Mildred Clore.
5. Catherine Huffman, born Bourbon County, Kentucky, 1802; married John Bradshaw.
6. Elijah Lyter Huffman, born 1805; died Louisville Kentucky, 1868. Married (1) Jerusha Ann Yeager; (2) Kate Crawford.
7. Sally Huffman, born 1807. Married Adam Miller.

The children of John Smith and Suzanne (Ament) Huffman were:

1. Amanda Fitzallen Huffman, born February 17, 1817 Bourbon County, Kentucky; died Collin County, Texas in 1897. Married Pierce Collier.
2. Henry Huffman, born in Bourbon County, Kentucky 1919; died in his youth.
3. Philip Ament Huffman, born Bourbon County, Kentucky, November 11, 1821; died in Forth Worth after 1890. Married in Shelby County, Kentucky in 1841, Caroline Crook.
4. Catherine Huffman, born at Floydsburg, Kentucky in 1823. Married Dr. Freeman.
5. JOHN SMITH HUFFMAN, JR., born Bourbon County, Kentucky, May 7, 1824; died June 22, 1865. Married in 1848 Mary Elizabeth Perrin, (born Russellville, Kentucky, June 27, 1826; died Merkel, Texas, July 12, 1916). Surgeon in the Confederate army.
6. Elijah Lyter Huffman, born in Bourbon County, Kentucky, September 25, 1827; died in San Angelo, Texas, May 29, 1913. Married Elizabeth Talkington in 1861.
7. Mary Huffman (twin), born Bourbon County, Kentucky, May 5, 1830; died Plano, Texas, March 13, 1912. Married Silas Harrington.
8. Martha Huffman (twin), born Bourbon County, Kentucky, May 5, 1830; died in 1864. Married (1) Alfred Harrington; (2) Moses Moore.

The children of John Smith Huffman and Lucinda (Armstrong) Huffman:

1. Louise Armstrong Huffman, born June 3, 1832; died August 20, 1882. Married November 8, 1856, Francis Marion Dougherty.
2. Ella Huffman, born 1834. Married Calvin Holmes.

3. William Gunn Huffman, born August 23, 1836; died April 13, 1862, Collin County, Texas.
4. Rebekah Means Huffman, born 1839. Married (1) Leigh Oldham, (2) Henderson Holmes.
5. Lucy Huffman, born 1841. Married William Holmes.

The children of John Smith Huffman Jr. and Mary Elizabeth (Perrin) Huffman were:

1. Laura Catherine Huffman, born Collin County, Texas, November 1, 1849; died McKinney, Texas, 1928. Married Isaac T. Largent January 1, 1867.
2. Sue E. Huffman, born Collin County, Texas, 1850; died January 4, 1927 at Polson, Montana. Married William H. Noel November 20, 1867.
3. John Ellen Huffman, born December 25, 1851; died March 30, 1930, McKinney, Texas. Married John Allen.
4. Ella Huffman, born February 27, 1853; died May 3, 1912. Married George W. Gallup in 1875.
5. RUTH AMENT HUFFMAN, born December 10, 1854, Collin County, Texas; died February 14, 1936. Married Joseph Wilson Baines (born January 24, 1846; died November 18, 1906) on September 12, 1869.
6. Mary Amanda Huffman, born Collin County, Texas, March 22, 1857. Married Lewis Sloane.
7. Carrie Liter Huffman, born March 27, 1858; died Houston, Texas, March 20, 1914. Graduated from Christian College, Columbia, Missouri and later taught school. Married Sam Houston Sterling in Anahuac, Texas, April 29, 1882.
8. Martha Rebekah Means Huffman, born May 29, 1859, Collin County, Texas; died March 2, 1939, Blanco, Texas. Married Charles Bowden Browning in Blanco, Texas.
9. William Gunn Huffman, born January 5, 1861; died May 1, 1920. Married Alene O'Neal, Dallas, Texas.
10. Lula Huffman, born October 4, 1863; died December 17, 1949 at McKinney, Texas. Married Charles M. Largent.

The children of Laura Catherine Huffman Largent and Isaac T. Largent were:

1. John Thomas Largent, born October 11, 1868; died November 25, 1886, Melissa, Texas.
2. Minnie Largent, born February 22, 1870; died February 25, 1870.
3. Myrtie F. Largent, born August 5, 1872; died March 26, 1904, McKinney, Texas.
4. Edmund J. Largent, born May 13, 1874; died 1938, McKinney, Texas.
5. Ruth L. Largent, born October 16, 1877; died McKinney, Texas.
6. Roy Isaac Largent, born September 28, 1879; died September 26, 1943, McKinney, Texas. Married October 12, 1904, Bessie Hamilton, born March 24, 1882.
7. Mary Amanda Largent ("Coochie"), born October 8, 1883; died May 9, 1897.

The children of Sue Huffman Noel and William H. Noel were:

1. Mary Lula Noel, born 1870, McDonald County, Missouri; died December 10, 1892. (See pages 106–111, "Illustrated History of McDonald County, Missouri," author, J. A. Sturges.)
2. Laura Noel, born 1872; married Sidney Holly.
3. Lee Noel, born 1874; died age nineteen.
4. Minnie Noel, born 1878. Married (1) Thomas Spencer, (2) J. C. Macomber, Seattle, Washington.
5. Walter Noel, born 1880, lives in Watervliet, N.Y.
6. Scott Noel, born 1882, lives in Peoria, Arizona.
7. Lora Noel, born July 10, 1884; died May 5, 1949. Married V. L. Holding, lived in Montana and California.
8. Noma Noel, born 1886; died at about six years of age.
9. Clay Noel, born 1888; married Alice Upton, lived in Oklahoma.
10. Wilda Noel, born 1890; married Ross Collison.

The children of John Ellen Huffman and John Allen were:

1. William Huffman Allen, born April 9, 1874 in Collin County, Texas; died July 28, 1953 in San Antonio, Texas. Lawyer.
2. Rose Allen, born 1876; died 1928. Schoolteacher in Collin County.
3. Lillie Lula Allen, born 1878; married Frank Gurney.
4. Carrie Ella Allen, born June 6, 1880; married Robert Duncan, April 17, 1901.
5. Laura Sue Allen, born 1887. Taught school for a number of years in McKinney.

Children of Ella Huffman Gallup and George W. Gallup were:

1. Rebecca Gallup, born in Collin County, Texas, October 28, 1878; died September 1925, at Oklahoma City, Oklahoma. Married Andy Goodwin, Crowell, Texas in January 1900.
2. Lucy Gallup, born Collin County, Texas, September 30, 1880; died at Swearingen, Texas, January 31, 1952. Married Egbert Fish, June 29, 1904.
3. Ella Amanda Gallup, born Collin County, Texas, January 10, 1883; died January 2, 1945 at Goodlet, Texas. Married W. L. Wilson May 3, 1905, who died January 31, 1952.
4. George W. Gallup, born Collin County, Texas, March 1, 1885; died January 1938 at Los Angeles, California. Married Lillian Davis, Wichita Falls, Texas, about 1923.
5. Laura Gallup, born Collin County, Texas, May 6, 1886; died May 16, 1952. Married Arthur W. Keller, Crowell, Texas, 1917.
6. Willie Lou Gallup, born Collin County, Texas, May 27, 1889; died December 1918. Married Walter Carr, Crowell, Texas about 1906.
7. Johnnie Anna Gallup, born Collin County, Texas, June 5, 1892. Married (1) Jack Davis, Crowell, Texas, (2) V. W. Matthews, May 26, 1926; resides at Lubbock, Texas.

Children of RUTH AMENT HUFFMAN BAINES and Joseph W. Baines:

1. REBEKAH BAINES, born June 26, 1881, McKinney, Texas. Married August 20, 1907 SAM EALY JOHNSON (October 11,

1877–October 22, 1937) at Fredericksburg, Texas. Resides at Austin, Texas.

2. Huffman Baines, born April 7, 1884, Austin, Texas. Married (1) Dora Marsh on June 19, 1909, (2) Ovilee Bogardus, June, 1942.
3. Josefa Baines, born May 21, 1889, Blanco, Texas. Married William Edgar Saunders, May 21, 1909. Resides at San Antonio, Texas.

Children of Mary Amanda Huffman Sloane and Lewis Sloane were:
1. Ruth Baines Sloane, born January 26, 1889, Blanco, Texas. Married Jones P. Popham, November 19, 1907 at Humble, Texas.
2. Mary Lou Sloane, born at Crowley, Louisiana, November 9, 1890. Married Julian B. Conner at Humble, Texas on February 23, 1911.
3. Martha Rebecca Sloane, born Crowley, Louisiana, March 17, 1893. Married John Adam Sons on June 21, 1913.
4. Jerry Simpson Sloane, born Crowley, Louisiana, March 3, 1895. Married Jewel Jones on February 3, 1935.
5. Lewis Lloyd Sloane, born Crowley, Louisiana, November 25, 1897.

Children of Carrie Liter Huffman Sterling and S. H. Sterling:
1. Hulon Sterling, born at Anahuac, Texas about 1884.
2. Philip Huffman Sterling, born 1888.
3. Benjamin Franklin Sterling, born Anahuac, Texas on November 14, 1893. Married August 21, 1923 to Helen Elizabeth Neumann (born Houston, Texas, February 21, 1905). Reside at Houston, Texas.

Children of Martha Rebekah Means Huffman Browning and Charles B. Browning (April 7, 1853–Feb. 27, 1948) were:
1. Eugene Baines Browning, born Blanco, Texas, October 10, 1889; died March 12, 1952. Married Mary Cage.
2. Ruth Browning, born September 9, 1893, Blanco, Texas. Married Joe Buckner on October 13, 1911, Blanco, Texas. Resides at Blanco, Texas.

Children of William Gunn and Alene O'Neal Huffman were:
1. Reina Allene Huffman, born April 1, 1892. Married (1) _____ (2) Barry Kelley
2. William Gunn Huffman, Jr., born February 5, 1891.
3. Ruth Huffman, born   ; died   . Married _____ Whiting. Children were Ann Barry Whiting and Reina Allene Whiting.

Children of Lula Huffman Largent and Charles M. Largent were:
1. Thomas Huffman Largent, born Merkel, Texas, July 12, 1889. Married Velma Sutphen.
2. Willie Joe Largent, born February 22, 1892. Married Clara Mae Saffle.
3. Leno Perrin Largent, born February 16, 1895. Married Luther Lycurgus Swofford.
4. Roy Rust Largent, born December 6, 1902. Married Hazel Harkrider.
5. Charles Marcus Largent, Jr., born March 16, 1909. Married Bertha Mae Rogers.

Desha Line

Robert Desha I married Elinor Wheeler

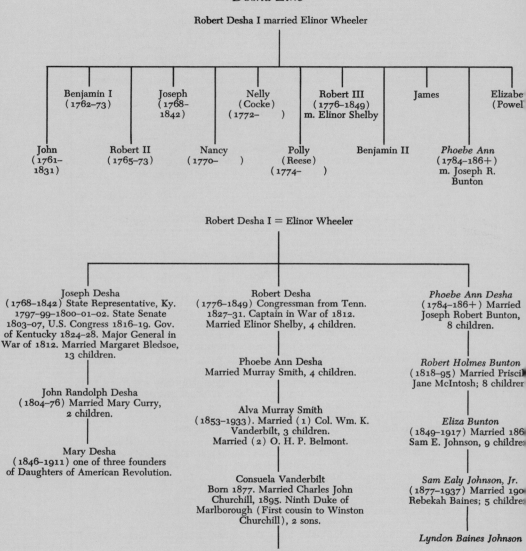

Benjamin I (1762–73)	Joseph (1768–1842)	Nelly (Cocke) (1772–)	Robert III (1776–1849) m. Elinor Shelby	James	Elizabe (Powel
John (1761–1831)	Robert II (1765–73)	Nancy (1770–)	Polly (Reese) (1774–)	Benjamin II	*Phoebe Ann* (1784–186+) m. Joseph R. Bunton

Robert Desha I = Elinor Wheeler

Joseph Desha
(1768–1842) State Representative, Ky.
1797–99–1800–01–02. State Senate
1803–07, U.S. Congress 1816–19. Gov.
of Kentucky 1824–28. Major General in
War of 1812. Married Margaret Bledsoe,
13 children.

John Randolph Desha
(1804–76) Married Mary Curry,
2 children.

Mary Desha
(1846–1911) one of three founders
of Daughters of American Revolution.

Robert Desha
(1776–1849) Congressman from Tenn.
1827–31. Captain in War of 1812.
Married Elinor Shelby, 4 children.

Phoebe Ann Desha
Married Murray Smith, 4 children.

Alva Murray Smith
(1853–1933). Married (1) Col. Wm. K.
Vanderbilt, 3 children.
Married (2) O. H. P. Belmont.

Consuela Vanderbilt
Born 1877. Married Charles John
Churchill, 1895. Ninth Duke of
Marlborough (First cousin to Winston
Churchill), 2 sons.

John Albert Spencer Churchill
Ivor Charles Spencer Churchill

Phoebe Ann Desha
(1784–186+) Married
Joseph Robert Bunton,
8 children.

Robert Holmes Bunton
(1818–95) Married Priscil
Jane McIntosh; 8 childrer

Eliza Bunton
(1849–1917) Married 186
Sam E. Johnson, 9 childre

Sam Ealy Johnson, Jr.
(1877–1937) Married 190
Rebekah Baines; 5 childre

Lyndon Baines Johnson

Jameson—Perrin Line

Line of Mary Elizabeth Perrin Huffman.

1. Alexander Jameson, 1650 lived near Glasgow, Scotland. His son:
2. James Jameson, married Scotch girl. Had twin sons, Robert and:
3. John Jameson, settled on Susquehanna River below Philadelphia. His son:
4. Thomas Jameson, born November 7, 1732; died April 6, 1823. In Revolutionary service. Married Hannah Taggart in Lancaster, Pennsylvania. Their daughter was:
5. Catherine Jameson, born August 20, 1773, Franklin County, Virginia. Married in 1792 at Russellville, Kentucky, Charles Perrin, who died in 1850. Their son was:
6. William Perrin, born October 15, 1800; married Dicea Kerby in 1820. Moved to Collin County, Texas. Their daughter:
7. Mary Elizabeth Perrin, born Russellville, Kentucky, June 26, 1826; married in Collin County in 1848, Dr. John Smith Huffman, surgeon in the Confederate Army, born May 7, 1824, Kentucky; died June 22, 1865. Came to Texas in 1846. Their daughter:
8. Ruth Ament Huffman, born December 10, 1854, Collin County, Texas. Married September 12, 1869, Joseph Wilson Baines; died February 13, 1936, San Antonio, Texas. Her daughter:
9. Rebekah Baines, born June 26, 1881, McKinney, Texas. Married Sam Ealy Johnson, Jr., August 20, 1907. Their son:
10. Lyndon Baines Johnson.

The Jamesons

I. ALEXANDER JAMESON, lived six miles from Glasgow, Scotland. His son:

II. JAMES JAMESON, lived at the same place in 1675. During the Persecution he went to Londonderry, Ireland, where he married a Scotch girl. She died leaving twin sons, who were ten years old. These sons, Robert and:

III. JOHN JAMESON, came to the American Colonies with their father and landed on the Susquehanna River below Philadelphia. John reared four sons; the second son:

IV. THOMAS JAMESON, born November 7, 1732; died Jefferson County, Indiana, 1823. Resided in Albemarle and Franklin Counties, Virginia. Thomas had belonged to the Virginia Militia and had taken the oath of allegiance to King George of England, but he and his three eldest sons joined the American Revolution. He was a corporal in charge of four scouts. He was well acquainted with General Washington and was within twenty steps of him when Cornwallis surrendered. He first married Jane Dickey (1742–1763) and moved to Georgia. They had four children: Samuel, John, Martha, and William Jameson. Thomas married in Lancaster, Pennsylvania in 1764, Hannah Taggart, born in Ireland, April 2, 1745; died January 10, 1834. Their ten children were:

   1. Mary Jameson, born October 10, 1766. Married Thomas Skelton.

2. Jane Jameson, born 1768; married (1) Abner Bird; (2) Isaac Davis.
3. Nancy Jameson, born 1770; married John Holcombe.
4. CATHERINE JAMESON, born 1773; married in Russellville, Kentucky, 1792, Charles Perrin who died there in 1850.
5. Eleanor (Helen) Jameson, born 1775; died 1816. Married in Franklin County, Virginia, October 10, 1795, George Kerby.
6. Margaret Jameson, born October 7, 1779; married Samuel Glasgow.
7. Alexander Jameson, born 1781; died in 1860. Married (1) Mary Moore; (2) Rachel Tenn; (3) Catherine Huffman.
8. Thomas Jameson, born May 10, 1783; died June 27, 1843. Married October 12, 1809, Sallie Humphreys.
9. Hannah Jameson, born August 22, 1787; died February 3, 1865. Married September 16, 1806, Samuel Ross.
10. Rhoda Jameson, born 1790; died September 1866. Married Samuel Humphreys.

Children of Catherine Jameson and Charles Perrin were:

1. Abner Perrin, born Logan County, Kentucky, April 6, 1797; died there as a young man, single.
2. Elizabeth Perrin, married James Sayle. Had children: America, Eliza, James and Thomas, twins.
3. WILLIAM PERRIN, born Logan County, Kentucky, October 15, 1800; died Collin County, Texas in 1856. Was Peters' colonist. Married Dicea Kerbey, born 1798.
4. Thomas Jameson Perrin, born July 21, 1805; died Cook County, Texas, 1878. Married (1) Jane Travis; (2) Euphemia Travis; (3) Ann Simpson. Had children, Ben, Elizabeth, Elvira, Jane and Caroline.
5. George Jameson, born 1807.
6. John Perrin, born December 16, 1809; died August 4, 1848. Married Miss Hockersmith; had four children; John, Hervey, Rice and Solon.
7. Dr. Isaac Newton Perrin, born May 28, 1810; married Louisa Ann Carney, January 29, 1839. Children were:
    1. James Madison Perrin, born June 18, 1841; killed by a horse in Lamar County, Texas, February 3, 1852.
    2. Christopher Columbus Perrin, born Lamar County, Texas, October 4, 1848; married Ella Carrie Braly, May 14, 1890.
    3. John Green Perrin, born February 9, 1850; died August 12, 1850.
    4. Dr. Galin C. Perrin, born February 12, 1852; died September 22, 1878. Married Nannie Braly, February 1877. A daughter:
        a. Annie Pearl Perrin, born November 10, 1877; died June 28, 1895.
    5. Stahl E. Perrin, born February 21, 1855; died Farmersville, Texas, in 1875.
8. James Madison Perrin, born Lamar County, Texas, October 2, 1813; married Tempie Ann Elizabeth Gardner. Their seven children were:
    1. Alford Curtis Perrin, born August 1842; died June 30,

1896. Married Frances Barbour. One daughter,
- a. Virginia May Perrin, born June 6, 1883. Graduated Grayson College and University of Texas, B.A. 1908.
2. Catherine Perrin, married A. J. Pogue, 1868. Children were:
- a. Madison Pogue, married Miss Hurley.
- b. Louisa Pogue, married Mr. Lackey.
3. Victoria Perrin, married S. R. Clifton; children were:
- a. Lizzie Clifton, who married Lawson Gill
- b. Maggie Clifton, who married an Anderson
- c. Katie Clifton
- d. Lora Clifton
- e. Hugh Clifton
4. Christopher C. Perrin, born on a Mississippi steamboat, December 1849; died Lamar County, Texas, September, 1852.
5. Susan Perrin, born 1852; married George Creecy. Children were:
- a. Margaret Creecy, married a Newton
- b. Lizzie Creecy, married a Gill
6. James Ed Perrin, married (1) Matilda Stevens; (2) Angeline Stephens. Children were:
- a. Curtis Perrin
- b. Tennie Perrin, married Herman Myers
- c. Bessie Perrin
- d. Alonzo Perrin
7. William Joseph Perrin.

Children of William and Dicea (Kerbey) Perrin were:
1. Abner Perrin, born about 1821, Girard County, Kentucky. Bachelor. Died in Collin County, Texas during the Civil War.
2. James Perrin, born about 1823. Married twice, had two sons: Robert Perrin, had children: Lyman, Minnie, Robert and Edna Lee Perrin
3. Catherine Perrin, born in 1824. Married John Bryan. Had two daughters:
- a. Louise Bryan, married William Speer
- b. America Bryan, married John Carson
4. MARY ELIZABETH PERRIN, born June 27, 1826, Russellville, Kentucky; died ____, McKinney, Texas. She came to Texas with her parents, Peters' colonists, settling in Collin County, Texas. There, in 1848, she married Dr. John Huffman. Their children were:
- a. Laura Catherine Huffman (Largent)
- b. Sue Huffman (Noel)
- c. John Ellen Huffman (Allen)
- d. Ella Huffman (Gallup)
- e. Ruth Ament Huffman (Baines)
- f. Mary Amanda Huffman (Sloane)
- g. Carrie Lyter Huffman (Sterling)

 h. Rebekah Means Huffman (Browning)

 i. William Gunn Huffman

 j. Lula Huffman (Largent)

5. Ellen Perrin, married Granville Thomas. Had two daughters.

6. George Perrin, killed by falling tree in Rowlett, Collin County, Texas. Had two daughters; Katie who married Jim Reger; Georgia Ann, who married B. Hill.

7. Charles Perrin, born   ; died Decatur, Texas in 1900. Married Mourning Finley. Their children were: Abner, born 1870, Dicea, Martha, Joshua, Noma, William, Melinda, John, Oma and Ethel.

8. Amanda Perrin, married Henry Clay Thomas. Had seven children; the eldest married Riley McMillan.

9. Anne Perrin, married four times.

10. William Perrin, married Tempie Largent. Had daughter, Dicea Perrin.